The History of Hampton and Richmond Borough Football Club

Vol 2: 2002-2021

All rights reserved. No part of this publication may be reproduced or transmitted in aby form or by any means, electronic or mechanical, including photocopy, recording or any other information storage and retrieval system, without prior knowledge or permission in writing from the authors.

Copyright © 2021 Tony Nash & Les Rance
All rights reserved.
ISBN: 9798717255486

CONTENTS

	Foreword – Jacques Le Bars	
1	Introduction	1
2	The Year of Three Managers 2002-03	4
3	Revival: Alan Devonshire 2003-11	11
4	The Supporters' Trust	38
5	The Austerity Years 2011-15	41
6	Dowson Unbound: 2015-18	59
7	Hampton and Richmond's Footballing Family	74
8	The McCann Years 2018-21	85
9	Appendix 1: League Tables	100
10	Appendix 2: Club Honours	110
11	Appendix 3: 100 Club	111

Foreword

When I was asked to write a foreword for this second volume of the History of Hampton and Richmond Borough Football Club, although delighted to oblige, I was also a little intimidated as the previous version of the club's history published in 2002 contained a foreword from Alan Simpson OBE.

As my Godfather, Alan was a huge influence in my life and even though I consider myself fairly competent with the written word, he had a bit more of a track record than me, besides which, he also had 45 odd years of memories and experiences following the Beavers home and away to draw upon. However, I have no choice but to start with a thank you to him. Without his obsession I would not have been sitting here writing this now. His introduction of me to the hidden, higgledy-piggledy, haven that is the Beveree came at an early age. An oasis of football in a corner of London dominated by the wrong shaped ball.

The date, opponent and result of whichever match was my first is a distant and long forgotten memory. At the time I was more interested in kicking a ball about on the pitch with proper goals after the final whistle. Indeed, not being local, I was not a frequent visitor to matches as a child. The odd one at the Bev when we visited Hampton. The occasional away game when it was close to my home in Kent. My main football fixes during my youth and into young adulthood were dominated by a love for Queens Park Rangers mixed with a shared season ticket at Charlton Athletic (where my friends were supporters) and regular visits to my local non-league side Bromley FC (where you could get a cheap pint at a not quite so legal age).

My father Philippe was a musician and writer and had no real interest in the game, so Alan was the font of football knowledge which was constantly bubbling away in the background. That meant Hampton FC as it was and Hampton and Richmond Borough FC as it became, was a constant in my life. A match report provided over Sunday lunch, a selection grievance aired over a glass of Burgundy or a breakdown of the exciting (and no doubt to prove not up to it later) new player during a game of chess ensured that Hampton was one of the first results I looked out for on a match day.

Despite that seed being planted, to now have the privilege of occupying the role of Chairman at this wonderful club is something I could never have predicted. Suddenly, listening to opinions on managers like Botley, Cordery and Devonshire has given way to making decisions alongside Dowson and McCann. Being a guest at playoff finals against Eastbourne Borough and Hayes & Yeading has been replaced with media interviews prior to the play-off final against Braintree Town and FA Cup games against Oldham Athletic. Times have indeed changed.

Alas it is not all fun and games, in my short time at the club we have encountered a huge number of challenges, not least the unprecedented situation the world faced when the Corona Virus pandemic hit in 2020. Whilst it has been an exceedingly difficult period, it has however highlighted to me the importance of this football club to its fans, staff and local community. It demonstrated the desire to support not only the club itself but those who really needed help during such hard times. Thankfully, it does appear that we are now coming out the other side and I suppose that brings with it a new period in the history of HRBFC. Perfect timing for the club's centenary season.

There is no doubt that the footballing landscape has changed hugely since our author Tony Nash first published his history of the club in 2002 and is even more unrecognisable compared to Alan's first experience of the Beveree in 1966. The game at non-league level now resembles far more the professional game, huge wage bills, full time players, sports science, academies, constant media coverage. It is all there. Yet somehow, we manage to retain the charm and intimacy of the non-league game. That ability to interact with the players and manager in Hammonds after a game, the importance of the Supporters Trust to the running and funding of the club and the input from our fans and volunteers who make Hampton & Richmond Borough FC what it is and enable it to run each and every day.

Whatever your memories of this great club, I hope you are, like me very proud of being part of it and even more importantly, looking forward to making future memories and being part of the history of this club for the next 100 years.

Thanks to Tony and Les for their dedication to this publication, to all those who have contributed to it and to you for reading it.

And as I always like to finish………. "Come on You Beavers!"

Jacques Le Bars
March 2021

Introduction

On the 25th May 2021 Hampton & Richmond Borough Football Club was 100 years old. A momentous milestone reached at an even more momentous time in world history with future of the national game beset by confusion and uncertainty brought about by the global pandemic of Covid 19. By the time you read these words you may find them completely out of date such have been the twists and turns of fortune since Covid struck in March 2020.

Hampton's centenary may fly well under the radar of national news coverage, but it is not a birthday that we intend to let pass without commemoration. This book is part of a series of tributes that hopefully will be played out over the 2021-2022 season and we hope you will enjoy remembering with us the ups and downs of the last twenty or so seasons starting with the low point of relegation in 2003 and ending in with,........well who knows what, under current manager Gary McCann in 2021.

Some of you will have read the original history published in 2002 which covered the first 80 years of the club's history. This second volume is just that, not a re-write or an update of the previous book, but a second instalment that brings the history bang up to date with events since then. The first instalment was not exactly a global best-seller (I still have a few copies left if anyone is interested!) but was never meant to be anything other than a labour of love. Since that publication there have been more than enough events on and off the field to merit a second volume on its own. We have also seen a collection of reminiscences, "This Thing of Ours" published in 2018 by long-time supporter Nick Levy which covered the supporter experience, a collective autobiography if you will. There are regular written pieces online and in the match day programme covering the club history and its characters so the bibliography of one smallish football club is growing by the day. This time I have been joined by the "Old Historian," Les Rance, who has chronicled the rise, fall and rise again of the club through numerous articles. Les is also the go-to man for records and statistics which one day will prove useful in that great Hampton FC pub quiz that I always imagined might happen when we reached 100 years of age. Third highest scorer in 1972-3? Les will know in an instant.

Les and I have shared the seasons between us and covered some of the other major developments at the club such the Academy, Ladies, Pan-Disability and Supporters' Trust which had not even been thought about back at the start of the century and are now an integral part of the club. We hope you will find it of interest and jog a few memories. Even researching the more recent seasons it is amazing just how many player's names you have forgotten, just how many you wish you had forgotten, and just how many of those were signed by Alan Dowson!

We start at the nadir with the cataclysmic relegation of 2003 quickly followed by the revival under Alan Devonshire which saw two promotions and three play-off finals, and which nearly resulted in Hampton reaching the top level of the non-league game. This was followed by relegation and some indifferent seasons as financial pressures weighed heavily on the club and country as a whole – the austerity years. With the arrival of Alan Dowson, the wheel turned once more as he dragged the club up by its bootstraps, going from success to success but agonisingly just falling short at that last play-off hurdle. Following a period of adjustment, the latest incumbent of the managerial hotseat, Gary McCann, has started to build another exciting side perhaps capable of making that last step up but cruelly undermined by the arrival of the global pandemic. It would have been most fitting if we could have celebrated with another promotion as we enter our centenary season but even Gary couldn't find the tactics to beat a global pandemic so we will have to wait and dream on a little longer.

Just a word on naming conventions. We use "Hampton" to refer Hampton and Richmond Borough FC throughout. Saves a lot of typing! Thanks go to Chris Hurst for his extensive photo and articles library, and numerous club photographers including Thom Lang, Laura Brain and Ben Harrison for additional photos which we have dipped into as well as Les' own archive. Some we simply have not been able to trace so apologies if we have missed you out.

Tony & Les
1 August 2021

The Year of Three Managers

Isthmian League Premier Division: 2002-03 Season

It is far too common an occurrence in non-league football that change at the top brings about wholesale changes throughout the club. And so it was to prove for Hampton as they experienced one of the most difficult seasons in their recent history. The 2001/02 season had ended in grim disappointment and recrimination. Hampton finished third from last in the Isthmian Premier Division, fortunate that only one team were relegated that season. The money had run out and so had the manager and Chairman, albeit in quite different directions.

2002/03 was to be Hampton's fifth season in the Isthmian Premier, their best finish having been 9th place. It must be remembered that the Isthmian Premier was then a direct feeder into the Conference National League, then known as the Nationwide Conference, so the quality of opposition was significantly stronger than the Isthmian League today. Teams such as Sutton Utd, Gravesend & Northfleet (now Ebbsfleet), Aldershot Town and Boreham Wood were all members at that time. During the next couple of years, the national league system underwent major restructuring which, if clubs were not careful, could push them well down the pyramid and a lot further away from the top step.

The departure of club Chairman, Vic Searle, at the end of the previous season so soon after the resignation of manager Steve Cordery, left the Committee having to find new leadership on and off the field. Mike Holland stepped up to become interim Chairman and started the process of advertising for a new manager. With the close season recruitment period already under way he needed to find a new manager at short notice at the same time as working out

Ian McDonald

what could be offered as a playing budget. There had been some speculation that Cordery's right-hand man and fan favourite, Craig Maskell, might step up the role but those plans were quickly dashed when Maskell, predictably, joined Cordery at Isthmian Premier division rivals, Aylesbury Utd. Cordery's team had already broken up over the course of the 2001-02 season as money pressures took their toll so it was not surprising that most players took the opportunity to move on to pastures new.

Some continuity was maintained when team sponsor and local property developer, Mervyn Cox, agreed to become Chairman. A new manager was found in the shape of ex-Aldershot manager, 49-year-old Ian McDonald, who came strongly recommended by former Woking manager Geoff Chappell who had McDonald as his assistant at Conference side Kingstonian. McDonald was a well-qualified coach holding a UEFA A licence and plenty of experience as a player in the professional game mainly in the lower divisions ending up with over 350 games for Aldershot. When Aldershot imploded in 1992, McDonald had the unenviable task of being their last manager, albeit in a caretaking capacity, before the club finally collapsed. McDonald brought in Matt Beard who he knew from his time at Kingstonian as his assistant manager. Beard much later was to become manager of West Ham United Ladies. The hand dealt to McDonald by the Committee was not a strong one as the financial pressures of the previous seasons meant that the budget was roughly a third of what Cordery had at his disposal, returning Hampton to the levels of Isthmian Division South 1 days. Survival was going to be a tough task.

For McDonald it was a case of recruiting almost an entirely new side with only defenders Aiden O'Brien and Ronnie Girvan, fringe strikers Esyas Yhdego and Enrico Grimm, and midfielder Dudley Gardner returning from the previous season's squad. Girvan and Fiston Manuella were the only two players still under contract but wanted to move on, Girvan eventually joining Farnborough and Manuella[1] joining Aylesbury. McDonald, however, was hopeful of signing some more experienced players from his Kingstonian contacts:

"I am now hopeful of being able to sign four experienced players", McDonald told the local press. *"They could include some of those who were with me when I was assistant manager of Kingstonian, centre-half Eddie Saunders, wide-man Dean Thompson and strikers Eddie Akuamoah and Dean Thomas.*
"Last season Saunders was in the Conference with Woking, while Akuamoah was at Sutton and Thomas at Carshalton. If I can sign them it will give us a great chance of having a reasonably successful season."

Ex K's keeper Steve Farelly had agreed to join but then, disappointingly, switched to Woking, presumably having secured a better offer. Following a few friendlies, McDonald whittled down his squad to 21 players, although it would be fair to say some of those listed in the first home league programme were never to appear for the club. By necessity it was something of a scatter-gun approach. Of the formers K's players mentioned by McDonald only Dean Thomas signed, managing just three appearances before departing.

Amongst those for whom there were greater hopes, was exciting midfielder Ashley Sestanovich who looked a class above when on his game. Sestanovich had at one time been on Manchester City's books before embarking a peripatetic journey through some of Europe's lower professional leagues including Royal Antwerp and Mullinger Town in the League of Ireland. Midfielder Billy Mead, son of the former Millwall Chairman,

---

[1] Known in his Hampton days to be a bit hot-headed, Manuella was later gaoled for 2 months for head-butting a player during an FA Cup tie for Staines Town.

Andy Iga, a sometime spectacular shot stopper

Peter Mead, came in from Kingstonian as captain, free scoring forward David Cory from Walton and Hersham, goalkeeper Andy Iga from Whyteleafe and Northern Ireland former under 19 defender Gary McCraken who had been on the books at Fulham and Cambridge Utd. Promising young striker Lee Riddell from Farnborough was paired up with Dean Thomas. Midfielder Chris Rose also came in from Farnborough, one of the few players to last the course of the whole season. McDonald recruited 20 year old midfielder Alan Inns from Wokingham Town who, whilst not in the first choice starting line up to begin with, became one of the few genuine success stories of an otherwise difficult season.

League openers probably don't get much tougher than Sutton United at Gander Green Lane where all of Hampton's starting 11 were making their debuts. The Beavers put on a decent performance in the mid-summer heat against one of the fancied sides in the division but lost out to a first half goal by Mark Watson. There was some room for encouragement in the display and Hampton certainly looked competitive enough. The first home game on the following Tuesday night produced a 1-1 draw against Hayes when Sestanovich equalised with a late 30 yard piledriver showing just what a special talent he could be for the side. However, Hampton might have been buried by halftime if not for a number of great saves by Andy Iga in goal.

The first win, 1-0 over Bishops Stortford, did not arrive until the fifth league game when Lee Riddell's goal was the first time that Hampton had taken the lead in a game. They managed to hold on for the points despite heavy pressure from the visitors. This left Hampton a couple of places outside of the four relegation places on five points, by no means a disaster after seven games but a pattern was emerging that whilst defensively well-organised, goals were hard to come by with just four scored to date. This trend continued into September with narrow defeats by Harrow Borough and Bedford Town with only one goal scored in reply. Not surprisingly confidence was ebbing such that one report described the 3-0 away defeat at the hands of former manager Steve Cordery's Aylesbury Utd in late September as "abject and inept," Aylesbury cruising to a 3-0 half time lead and then easing off the gas. By the time the FA Cup 2nd Qualifying Round arrived to give some distraction from the league, Hampton had slipped into the bottom four having lost six out of 10 and scoring just five times, the lowest total in the division.

Guildford and Godalming of the Combined Counties League were the FA Cup opposition, themselves languishing at the bottom of their own division. Despite three steps difference Hampton made heavy weather of the game and were thankful for a Sestanovich 75th minute winner to progress to the next stage where they were drawn away to Slough Town of Isthmian League Division 1 South. Despite subsequently picking up a couple of points from draws it was clear that changes needed to be made to the squad and the Committee agreed a small increase in the budget to aid recruitment. However, Slough ran out easy winners in the Cup tie, 4-2, after another woeful display ended any further interest, and this was followed by a thoroughly depressing 2-0 defeat at fellow relegation candidates Enfield. By 21 September Hampton were bottom of the division. To a lack of goal threat was added a poor disciplinary and injury record such that four players missed the Enfield game due to suspension and three through injury. Iga was then red-carded at the end of the game for a handball outside his area which meant he was to miss the next game in the FA Trophy. McDonald was losing his patience and centre half O'Brien quit after a poor 3-1 home defeat by Chesham Utd. The manager reacted by ringing the changes for the visit of second placed Aldershot Town in the League, with nine changes to the line-up but despite a more spirited display Hampton lost 3-1 and dropped back to the bottom of the league.

With pressure mounting, Hampton next travelled on 2 November in the FA Trophy to Spalding Town, another side from a lower division struggling in last place in the Dr Martens Eastern Division making Hampton slight favourites - not that anyone was over-confident. With Iga suspended Chris Bouchez made his debut in goal and was unfortunately at fault in gifting Spalding a winner in a game where Hampton dominated possession without making chances count. It proved to be the last straw for the Committee who had already started to look at possible replacements for McDonald. Despite rumours that Geoff Chappell had been offered the job, the Committee, heavily persuaded by former Chairman Bob Hayes, moved swiftly to reappoint Chic Botley who had taken Hampton up to the Isthmian Premier four seasons earlier. The press release stated that McDonald had tendered his resignation, but it was clear that he had no other option and nor did the Committee. A record of one win in 17 league games, bottom of the table and just 8 goals scored was dismal by any measure. More controversial was whether Botley was the right man to lead the turnaround and undoubtedly there was an element of sentiment in the appointment. Since leaving Hampton he had managed without particular distinction at Banstead, Leatherhead and Molesey. Assistant Manager Matt Beard was

Chic Botley

keen to takeover but with the vacancy unadvertised Botley's appointment was a fait accompli. Beard soon moved on when Botley brought in his own assistants in former Beaver Robin Lewis and Reg Payne from Farnborough.

And what of Ian McDonald? Rightly regarded as an excellent coach, he struggled to recruit with a tiny budget and was not helped by injuries and suspensions to key players. It was clear from fairly early on that key man Sestanovich was looking for a move to a professional club and his performances apart from the occasional flash of brilliance did not show the consistency that was needed by his manager. Billy Mead, McDonald's captain, sustained a bad injury early on and failed to reappear. Suspensions abounded. New recruits showed no more quality than was already available.

Botley acknowledged his task in rescuing Hampton's league status was a big one but started out with a positive message. Finding some more strike power to address the chronic lack of goals however proved difficult with the budget dealt him. He persuaded left back Tony Houghton to return from Aylesbury and Richard O'Connor also returned for a second spell to bolster midfield. However, the miserable run continued with a particularly harrowing 6-0 defeat at Lewes in the League Cup described in the next programme notes as "the most inept and disgraceful performance in many a year." Botley then looked to former Beavers Del Bryan and Jesse Hall, whilst Darren Deegan returned at long last from the broken leg sustained in the FA Trophy game at Hereford in the previous season. Picking up a couple of points from draws made no real difference to the plight and by Christmas Hampton were well and truly adrift at the bottom. In a key relegation battle in early January against second bottom Ford Utd, Hampton lost by the odd goal in five. Remarkably Hampton got only their second win of the season with a 3-1 victory over former boss Steve Cordery's Aylesbury Utd, Sestanovich putting on a star performance as Hampton ran out 3-1 winners. There must have been scouts watching as it was to be his swansong for the Beavers. Shortly thereafter he signed for Stockport County following a two week trial although that deal quickly fell through and he ended up moving to Sheffield Utd, then in the old First Division (Championship) for a fee of £10,000 and promise of a first team friendly in the summer.[2]

Despite an ever-increasing flow of new signings, Botley could do no better than McDonald to stop the rot and the Committee finally lost patience with Botley in March appointing Brian Cottingham, who had replaced Robin Lewis as coach, as interim. Cottingham, who had played for Fulham in the 1980s, saw out the last eight games of the season which produced just one more win on the last day of the season at Billericay, Hampton's first away victory for 18 months. At least Cottingham installed some better team spirit in his short spell in charge and made himself a potential candidate for the role full time.

Botley's record was as poor as McDonald's with just one league win in 20 games and was enough to see him removed. But he further blotted his copy book when it came to light that he had forged four registration forms without the club's knowledge and was suspended by the league for four matches. The club fortunately avoided a fine or points deduction although that would have been academic given that they were already relegated. Botley was less than happy with the sacking. The local press quoted him as saying:

"The incident with the registration forms happened back in January. The four trialists in question were due to play in a low-key cup game. They had trained with us for four weeks and, as we did not have a reserve side, I just wanted to see the trialists play in a

---

[2] The fee was £3,000 plus a further £7,000 dependant on appearances. Ashley Sestanovich did not play first team football for Sheffield United but went out on loan to Scarborough and Grimsby Town. On and off field disciplinary incidents led to his contract being terminated and he drifted back down the leagues ending up at Farnborough Town and then Grays Athletic. In 2006 he was sentenced to eight years imprisonment for his part in a conspiracy to rob a South London roofing firm where a man was shot in the chest and subsequently died of injuries sustained.

competitive game. I made an error of judgement regarding the forms. Consequently, they never played for the club in the cup, and they were never registered to play for the club.

I was disciplined by the chairman Mr. Cox in January. The matter had been dealt with and was closed. There has been an apparent vendetta against me for some time and certain individuals have chosen to resurrect the matter for obvious reasons."

Botley took a pot shot at the running of the club Committee and claimed that there were financial problems. At this time Chairman Mervyn Cox also decided to step down citing work and family pressures with vice chairman, Mike Holland stepping up once again to cover whilst new leadership was sought. In truth Cox was not a big football supporter and was hands-off in the day to day running of the club. Understandably he was reluctant to pump in more funding when relegation was a certainty. The question now was Hampton destined to return to the relative obscurity of the early 1990s?

The final record made deeply dismal reading: 24th (and last place) Played 46, Won 3, Drew 14, Lost 29, Scored 35 Conceded 86, Goal difference -51, Points 23. Three wins matched Kingstonian's previous worst record from the 1978/79 season. 23rd placed Enfield finished 18 points ahead. It was the lowest number of goals scored in the division and the second worst defensive record. Top scorer was Lee Riddell on 10. Hampton were relegated to Isthmian League Division 1 South for the forthcoming 2003-4 season. Aldershot Town were the runaway champions and were promoted to the Conference National.

Chesham, Boreham Wood and Enfield were all relegated alongside Hampton.

They say never go back and in hindsight the reappointment of Botley was a mistake heavily influenced by sentiment for what he had previously achieved and the urgency to make a change from a disastrous start. His record since leaving Hampton the first time around might have suggested other candidates should have been considered but with the budget available it is doubtful that Hampton would have stayed up. The more pressing question was now whether new leadership could be found both on and off the pitch.

Press Officer (and co-author of this book), Les Rance, summed up the season in philosophical fashion: "I know relegation is a bitter pill to swallow, but it isn't the end of the world – it's just a new beginning." And he couldn't have been more prescient in his comments.

Ian McDonald later went on to manage at Farnborough under former Hampton Chairman Vic Searle. Farnborough was another crisis club that eventually collapsed and reformed. Aldershot, Kingstonian, Farnborough – all suffered a similar fate, not that McDonald was in any way responsible for their financial state, but he did seem to have the knack of being in the wrong place at the wrong time. He later returned to his native Cumbria and briefly managed his first club Workington Town.

Managers' Records

	P	W	D	L	F	A	Pts	Ave	Win %
Ian MCDONALD									
Combined	20	2	5	13	12	32			10.0
League	17	1	5	11	8	26	8	0.47	5.9
Cup	3	1	0	2	4	6			
Chic BOTLEY									
Combined	26	5	7	14	29	59			19.2
League	20	1	7	12	20	45	10	0.5	5.0
Cup	6	4	0	2	9	14			
Brian COTTINGHAM									
Combined	10	1	2	7	8	17	5	0.5	10.0

Revival: Alan Devonshire 2003-2011

Isthmian League Division 1 South: 2003/04 Season

Timing can sometimes work for you or against you. In Hampton's case two bits of good luck came together towards the end of the previous season. First, the return to the UK of former committee member Graham Wood and in April the announcement that Maidenhead manager, Alan Devonshire had decided to step down from the end of the 2002/03 season.

Graham Wood, a proud native of Gateshead, had been a committee member and sponsor in the 1970's but his business interests took him away from the South East and he had become involved as director and vice-chairman of Sunderland for a number of years. Then having sold his Doncaster based boiler-making business, he moved out to the United States to run its US subsidiary which he subsequently sold a few years later. He kept in touch with club President, Alan Simpson, and was spotted attending one or two Hampton games and it was not long before two and two were put together. At the same time Graham was also looking to help his boyhood club Gateshead who had fallen on hard times following the withdrawal of their key sponsor and subsequent years would see Graham drawn between the two sides. Whilst living in London, it was Hampton who were fortunate to get his backing and Graham agreed to become Chairman once the club had converted from a members' club to a new limited company. This project had been long in the pipeline the previous season but eventually was agreed in the late Spring of 2003 with Graham Wood, Alan Simpson and Mervyn Cox appointed as the three original directors.

Alan Devonshire

The Manager position was advertised with Alan Devonshire being the outstanding candidate. Alan's football career was an illustrious one playing 358 games for West Ham Utd and 8 Caps for England. He was a FA Cup winner in 1980 when Division 2 (that's old money Division 2) side West Ham beat Arsenal 1-0 at Wembley and was renowned as stylish attacking midfielder very much in the West Ham Academy mould. However, his early career saw him released from Crystal Palace as a youngster before joining Southall, then in the Athenian League, where he attracted scouts from a number of clubs before signing for West Ham in 1976 for a fee of £5,000. Alan knew first-hand how bruising the non-league game could be and adapted quickly to the physical demands of the professional game. After a persistent knee injury saw him quit football in 1992, for a while he managed Hampton Ladies team before establishing his reputation in the men's game at Maidenhead Utd from 1996 until he joined Hampton. At this time Maidenhead were members of the Isthmian Premier Division so joining Hampton was a step down the pyramid. His appointment as Hampton Manager was announced on 1st July. A few weeks later he was introduced to Supporters at a Q & A evening in the Clubhouse.

Most of the previous season's players had already left the club leaving it bereft of players. Caretaker Manager, Brian

Alan between Chief Executive Mike Holland and Club President Alan Simpson OBE

Cottingham, had joined Dorking, whilst some of the previous season's playing staff had already found new homes. Stuart Harte had joined Met Police; Tony Houghton had re-joined Dulwich Hamlet; Scott Bennetts had fetched up with AFC Wimbledon. In essence Devonshire was left with just a few loyal players.

Not surprisingly Devonshire dipped heavily into his Maidenhead set up bringing in assistant Carl Taylor as his No2 and a number of former Maidenhead teammates, Adrian Allen, Lee Channell, Marcelo Fernandez, Orlando Jeffrey, Andy Morley, Paul Kelly, Obinna Ulasi, Eric Kwayke and Craig Webster. To this was added experienced keeper Adrian Blake, defenders Rob Paris and Jamie Jarvis, midfielder Richie O'Connor back for another spell, plus striker Chris Stowe and right back Steve Omonua. From the previous season only Alan Inns, Dudley Gardner and Sam Okafor made the cut.

On paper it was a very strong squad and much fancied to bounce straight back to the Premier Division. The task in hand was also made easier by the reorganisation of the non-league system at the end of the 2003-04 season which was to see the creation of the new Conference North and South divisions feeding into the Conference National. This meant that six teams would each be promoted from Divisions 1 South and North to create a new Isthmian Premier which was shorn of its top 12 teams which moved into the new Conference South. In a quirk of the reorganisation each winner of the Division 1 South and North leagues was due to go into a series of play offs for a place in the Conference South, in effect a potential double promotion.

After a pre-season that included attractive games against AFC Wimbledon and Sheffield United, amongst others, the first competitive fixture was away to near-neighbours, Ashford Town (Middx). A dour 0-0 draw ensued; the main interest was the number of new faces on show – 12 of the 16 names on the team sheet were newcomers to the club.

Expectations were perhaps somewhat higher given the calibre of the players recruited. Most of the team had finished in 10th place in the Isthmian Premier whilst playing for

Maidenhead the season before. They would finish in 5th place, five points clear of 7th placed Dulwich Hamlet on 89 points. Hampton did spend quite a few months in 3rd or 4th but were never seriously challenged for the top spot, occupied by Lewes who finished five points ahead[3]. Lewes were promoted straight into the Conference South after winning their play-off games whilst Worthing (2nd), Windsor & Eton (3rd), Slough Town (4th) and Staines Town (6th) joined Hampton in the Isthmian Premier. Dulwich Hamlet (7th) lost out to Wealdstone in their play-off final and took their place in next season's re-vamped Isthmian Division One.

League highlights of the season were a 4-0 home win over Slough Town, a 7 goal thriller at Beveree in mid-January when Lewes were beaten 4-3, and a 4-1 win away at Whyteleafe. In the F A Cup wins were recorded against Great Wakering Rovers (3-0), Dunstable Town (1-0), Kingstonian (2-1), in front of a 560 home crowd – the best of the season- before losing at Paulton Rovers (1-2) in the 3rd Qualifying Round. It was not a happy trip to the West Country, Adrian Allen, Rob Paris and Paul Kelly were missing due to illness or injury whilst, on the coach trip, Jamie Jarvis and Alan Inns were both unwell, although both played.

The F A Trophy saw a quick exit. A 1-1 draw was secured at Arlesey Town, but the tables were turned when the visitors won 2-0 in the replay.

The Middlesex Senior Cup was exited at the Quarter Final stage in early February at home to Combined Counties, Bedfont. Bedfont levelled the score at 2-2 in the last minute and after a period of extra time, the lower ranked team won 5-3 on penalties. Former club stalwart, Steve Cheshire, returned after five years away to lead Bedfont into the semi-finals – needless to say he was applauded off the pitch in recognition of his previous service with the Beavers.

Another penalty shoot-out at Harefield saw the team exit the Middlesex Charity Cup at the Quarter-Final Stage, after a 1-1 draw failed to separate the teams.

Hampton had better luck in the Isthmian League Cup (sponsored by Bryco) navigating their way past Dulwich Hamlet (on penalties, after an exciting 3-3- draw), Leyton (2-1), Wingate & Finchley (4-2) and a quarter-final win at Bracknell Town (2-1). The run ended at the semi-final stage when Dunstable Town won the first leg 2-1 on their own patch, before cementing their appearance in the final with a 3-1 win at the Beveree.

63 matches were played in 2003/04. Andy Morley made 56 starts, Paul Kelly 55 appearances (52 +3 subs), Adrian Blake, 51 starts, Orlando Jeffrey, 50 starts. The main scorers were Adrian Allen, 24; Richard O'Connor,16; Michael Currie,14 and Andy Morley, 13. Alan Inns who only started to get a regular starting place from October won three awards at the end of season dinner.

At the End of Season Awards Dinner, Graham Wood, Chairman, congratulated everyone….

"The first team's objective in 2003/04 was to gain promotion from the Ryman League Division One South against what we knew would be fierce competition. The other likely contenders for the top places lived up to expectations and, as our fingernails will testify, it took the full 46 games and 89 points to achieve success."

---

[3] Lewes were managed by Steve King who went on to have a long and successful career in non-league management. He had been interviewed for the vacant Hampton manager's job.

Isthmian League Premier Division: 2004/05 Season

Alan Devonshire had achieved his initial target in gaining promotion from Division 1 (South) and was now faced with a campaign in the Premier Division which had completely changed in character from 2002/03, following the FA's re-structuring. Only seven clubs remained from the previous season with Hampton being one of 15 new sides to join the division. The Beavers would be facing brand new opposition including Eastleigh, Salisbury City, Dover Athletic and Folkestone Invicta – all from the Southern League. During the summer supporters had been busy 'tarting up' the ground and a group of volunteers led by Chris Mulberry and Ken Mace had built a two-step terrace on the 'school' side.

Pre-season training had got underway on 26th June and around 90 hopefuls (attracted by Devonshire's reputation) had turned up at Beveree looking for a spot in the first team and the resurrected Suburban League reserve side under Michael Howe. Carl Taylor, Devonshire's right-hand man would quickly have rooted out anyone not up the task in front of them.

The Under 18 team, under manager, Mike Hollis, was looking for a third championship in five years and the Women's team were looking to improve on the previous season's runner-up placing.

Those who made it into the new squad were new keeper Kieran Drake, Craig Lewington, Matt Elverson, Dean Wells, Luke Fontana and Graham Harper. Wells had been released from Brentford after austerity measures forced the disbandment of their Reserve team set up. He would play over 300 games whilst 'Harps' would make almost 250 appearances. Harper had caught Devonshire's eye when scoring twice for Whyteleafe against Hampton the previous season. Youngsters like Tom Crosland, Abdul Osman[4] and Lee O'Leary were given opportunities. The majority of the previous season's successful team including Alan Inns, Orlando Jeffrey, Andy Morley, Dudley Gardner, Adrian Allen and Obinna Ulasi were all to the fore.

A good start was made in the league, after ten games (4 wins, 4 draws, 2 defeats) the team were in 7th place. A run of seven home wins in nine games pushed Hampton up to 3rd by mid-November but their away form was proving to be their Achilles heel with just one win in eight games.

"I don't know why our away form has been poor," said Devonshire, *"but five of our next six games are away from home, so we need to start winning to stay near the top."*

Nevertheless, after a 1-0 win over Dover Athletic (Ryan Ashe with a penalty) they hit top spot for the first time. The undefeated home run continued for 23 games but ended when Heybridge Swifts completed a season double over the Beavers in early March.

Unfortunately, Hampton could not sustain the form that took them to the top and results over the winter were mixed, drifting down to the lower end of the play off places. A budget cut was announced in early January with four players being released but the Beavers were able to maintain their challenge. As the business end of the season drew near, Hampton were in 5th with just one win needed from their last two games to secure the last play-off place.

---

[4] Osman never really established himself in the side making 9 appearances but later went on to a successful pro career via Northampton Town, Partick Thistle and Crewe Alexandra amongst others.

The Middlesex Senior Cup gave the Beavers a run all the way to the Final – but nothing could be that simple, as controversy marred their match against Yeading (played at Staines Town). Victories over Kingsbury Town (3-1), Ashford Town (Middx), (1-0), Uxbridge (2-0) and Harrow Borough in the semi-final (2-1) set up a final with Yeading (who would end up as Premier Division Champions) on Easter Monday, March 28th. Prior to the game the club informed the Middlesex FA that Yeading were fielding an illegible player (who had been signed after the semi-final, contrary to the competition rules). The Middlesex representatives refused to act on this information and even threatened to ask Alan Devonshire to leave the ground. The game went ahead with Yeading winning 2-1 (the player in question was surprisingly substituted before half-time!) and despite Yeading infringing the rules (which should have led to expulsion) the officials ordered a replay for Tuesday 26th April which Yeading won 3-1. Devonshire fielded a weakened side now further depleted by injuries to Adrian Allen, new striker Richard Pacquette and Graham Harper. The League clearly had to take priority.

Middlesex Senior Cup Final, first final team

The decision may have caused Hampton to miss out on a play-off place as the Beavers were obliged to play four games in seven days between Saturday April 23rd and 30th.

Two league games on the Saturdays, against Billericay Town and Tonbridge Angels; Yeading in the replayed final on the Tuesday, and on Thursday 28th an Isthmian League Cup Final against Slough Town. All four games were lost – but a single point from the two league games would have earned the Beavers a place in the play-offs. The last game of the League season was against already relegated Tonbridge Angels but despite having nothing but pride to play for, Tonbridge came out on top with a 3-2 win – a frustrating end to the league campaign.

Yeading were promoted as Champions with Eastleigh winning the play off final against Leyton. Local rivals Kingstonian finished a long way distant in last place and were relegated.[5]

Hampton exited the FA Cup at the 1st Qualifying Round stage, losing 2-0 at Histon, not an easy draw as Histon went on to win the Southern League Premier division. An inconsistent display was punished with goals in the second half.

The FA Trophy also saw an early exit to Conference (South) outfit Sutton United. Drawn at home, the game ended in a 1-1 draw (a memorable goal thanks to a 50 yard lob executed by Ryan Ashe). The replay the following Tuesday night went from bad to worse. Matt Elverson (broken nose) and Obinna Ulasi were unavailable; Ryan Ashe and Elliott Godfrey got stuck in traffic and were relegated to the subs bench. Sutton led after 6 minutes and then Luke Fontana was stretchered off. Sutton were 3-0 up before

---

[5] Kingstonian illustrate the dangers of not owning your own ground. In 2005 it was sold out from under the club to AFC Wimbledon by the then owner. They became tenants in their own ground before another sale of Kingsmeadow to Chelsea saw them homeless before sharing at Corinthian Casuals.

Alan Inns pulled one back but the coup-de-grace was applied by Sutton's Glenn Boosey.

Leading scorers this season were Ryan Ashe and Luke Fontana with 14 each, Adrian Allen made it into double figures with 10. Keeper Kieran Drake started all 61 games, Dean Wells played in 59 whilst Alan Inns played in 52.

On balance 2004/05 would be regarded as an excellent season; runners-up in two cup competitions and achieving the club's highest ever league finish. The failure to make the play offs at the last gasp was the only tinge of disappointment. The crowded last weeks of the season proved too much for a thin squad but Hampton were in a good place.

Isthmian League Premier Division: 2005/06

During the summer Hampton's Chairman, Graham Wood, left the club, Graham deciding to return to his native North East. The opportunity to take over as Gateshead's Chairman was too strong for him to turn down. Wood had never forgotten the hurt when Gateshead were voted out of the Football League in 1960 despite finishing third bottom, with Oldham Athletic and Hartlepool United beneath them. Peterborough United were voted in – nothing to do with being the furthermost norther club was it![6] Former Chairman, Bob Hayes, stepped in but, as he pointed out at the time, he would be looking for someone else to take on the role. A month into the new season and Bob Hayes unveiled David Cole as the new Chairman on 6th September. Cole, a former Director of the Mirror Group, had his own company MEM Retail Marketing Services and had been sponsoring the Stadium and Match Day Programme since the beginning of the previous season. Significantly more investment flowed into the club but as we will see in Chapter 4 the new foundations were largely built on sand.

Perhaps the most unusual appointment was that of a 'Club Chaplain'. Tim Healey, Minister of Hampton Baptist Church took on

Aaron Gilbert – photo Les Rance

the role to offer support to all the staff – and supporters (at a later time this role would be taken on by Paul Barker after Healey left the area). One of Tim's first duties was to pay a visit to 19 year-old Aaron Gilbert. Aaron had made a few appearances in the first team during the previous season and was involved in a car accident.

Aaron's last appearance had been in the replayed Middlesex Senior Cup Final against Yeading. Tragically Aaron was left in a wheelchair – for life.

Pre-season had got under way with the bulk of the previous season's squad in attendance plus the usual bunch of hopefuls looking to impress. The major announcement by Alan Devonshire was the signing of a new goalkeeper, Matt Lovett, from rivals Staines

---

[6] Gateshead were soon promoted to the Conference National and reached the Conference play-off final in 2014, losing to Cambridge Utd.

Town. Lovett was an established number '1' having played over 450 games for the Swans. Hampton supporters regarded it as an excellent signing. Lovett missed some of the pre-season but made his debut in the opening league game, at home to Walton & Hersham (a 2-0 win). Amongst those other newcomers who would have an influence on the team were legendary goal scorer, Lawrence Yaku, recruited from Maidenhead United who replaced Adrian Allen, who had moved on to Chelmsford City, and Luke Fontana who had joined Carshalton Athletic. Also joining were defenders Brian Connor and Rob Paris, both ex-Maidenhead alumni and midfielders Steve Sodje from Tonbridge, Kelvin McIntosh from Oxford City and Francis Quarm, from Dulwich Hamlet. Yaku was already one of the most prolific goal scorers in non-league football having netted 136 times for Northwood before joining Maidenhead where the goals kept on coming. A late signing was talented midfielder Elliott Godfrey who had been on the books at Watford.

The Beavers got off to a great start winning their opening seven games, scoring 17 goals, conceding just 3. Helped by a settled team Hampton were sitting top of the table, in fact they would keep the top spot until 10th December, 21 games into the season. Yaku was providing the scoring power, Rob Paris and Dean Wells were dominating at the centre of the defence in front of Lovett between the sticks.

At one point Hampton led the division by nine points but a run of three defeats in November saw that lead cut back to just goal difference over Fisher Athletic.

During this period the club had its biggest crowd for a match, to date. The visitors were AFC Wimbledon' just promoted, who, at the start of the game were in 6th place, five points behind the Beavers. The reborn club –

Alan Devonshire and Matt Lovett – photo Les Rance

not a continuation of Wimbledon FC – appeared to have the attitude that all they had to do was turn up and with their massive support, success was a given. On the night, in front of 2,520, it was Hampton who had the last word. Wes Daley gave the Dons a 25th minute lead. Two minutes into the second half Yaku was brought down twenty yards from goal by Don's skipper Steve Butler – Referee Eamonn Smith took the decision to send Butler off. Paris equalised following the resulting free kick and then on the hour Elliott Godfrey volleyed in the winner. It is worth pointing out here that AFC Wimbledon have never beaten the Beavers in a competitive match – much to the chagrin of their supporters. But then the Beavers lost at home in the FA Trophy 2-0 to lowly Newport IOW, the fourth time in a row that Hampton had been knocked out of the Trophy in the first round.

Hampton regained the top spot on Boxing Day but from then on inconsistency set in. Wins became draws and draws became defeats. On the way they went to Kingsmeadow for the return encounter with the Dons and won convincingly 4-0 in front of a 3,315 crowd – Yaku, Quarm, Godfrey, with a penalty, and Ryan Lake, also with a penalty sending the Beaver Patrol home in raptures. As with the previous win over Wimbledon pride came before a fall as the Beavers were then thrashed 5-0 at home by fellow promotion hopefuls, Heybridge Swifts. Home form was letting them down and a run of four home defeats saw them slip out of the top five for the first time. Manager Devonshire, who had recently extended his contract, was happy that his team were playing well enough to reach the play offs even if results weren't quite going their way. In the end his side clung on to 5th place, Hampton's highest ever finish, after securing a final day of the season win over Billericay Town. They had gained four more points than the previous season.

The play-offs beckoned for a place in the Conference South with a trip to second placed Heybridge Swifts for a semi-final match. After a 1-1 draw and extra time it was all down to a penalty shoot-out. The Beavers won 4-2 and then had to visit Fisher Athletic (who had seen off AFC Wimbledon) in a winner takes-all Final, played at Dulwich Hamlet's Champion Hill ground. Hampton were without injured defenders Dean Wells and Andy Morley and 'keeper Matt Lovett was suspended. Sadly, it was not to be, and Fisher saw the Beavers off, winning comfortably 3-0. So near, yet so far it would all have to be done again next season.

In the cup competitions the Beavers soon exited the F A Cup after a replay with Leatherhead and as mentioned, the F A Trophy to Newport (IOW), followed by the Isthmian League Cup, also losing to Fisher[7]. However, the team did make it to a second successive Middlesex Senior Cup Final. On this occasion the Beavers met Hayes at Harrow Borough after 120 minutes of scoreless inactivity, the cup was won 4-3 on penalties.

---

[7] Fisher really were the bogey side this season. Hampton lost both league games, League Cup and Play Off Final. They were wound up by HMRC after two seasons in the Conference South following the discovery of unpaid bills.

Matt Lovett only missed two games all season, making 54 appearances; Graham Harper and Elliott Godfrey, 51; Dean Wells, 50. Yaku scored 24 goals, Godfrey 14; Paris, the big defender, chipped in with 7.

Alan Devonshire had built a strong squad, but could they take the next step?

Isthmian League Premier Division: 2006/07 Season

In order to prepare for the new season a massive amount of work was carried out at Beveree. The pitch was completely re-furbished, and a sprinkler system was installed – no longer did the groundsman, Bob Morford, have to drag out hoses to water the pitch. The biggest expense was on the Club House. A building that had been little changed for 40 years was, during the summer completely gutted, the whole inside re-designed front to back and side to side.

Team photo in away kit 2006/07

New facilities for the players and management, and the interior – to be christened 'Hammonds Bar' and giving the appearance of a 'swanky' Wine Bar. In all an estimated £200k had been spent by the new Chairman.

Just one problem – no Boardroom to entertain visiting officials. The club would have to manage the rest of the season partitioning part of the Club House until a new facility could be brought in. The pitch was perfect, and the facilities were uprated – now could the team respond?

The majority of the squad remained from the previous season, in fact 17 players were still with the club. The main newcomer was 26-year-old Cornish born, Ian Hodges who had played for Hayes in the Conference South. Ian came with a reputation both for scoring goals and making the lives of opposing defenders as difficult as possible. For the next five seasons, Hodges would make the number 9 shirt his own.

A good pre-season enabled Hodges to build up a striking partnership with the experienced Lawrence Yaku. The squad had relatively few additions to the previous season, early newbies were Glen Harris, in August; Marvin Bartley[8] from Didcot Town, October, and in February, Stuart Lake who joined his brother, Ryan, who had joined almost a year earlier (both from Ashford Town (Middx). Stuart Lake had a reputation as a bit of 'hard' player but in his time with the Beavers showed himself to be an exciting midfield player, a scorer of important goals and extremely popular with the supporters.

In the league the team got off to a good start winning at East Thurrock and home to Hendon, Hodges scoring four out of the five goals (incidentally, Hendon were managed by a certain Gary McCann, who would become manager of the Beavers in 2018). After those early victories results became somewhat mixed and by mid-November the team had slumped to 14th spot and seemingly drifting. There was an early exit in the Trophy at Windsor & Eton, 2-0, Hampton missing a hatful of chances and then a penalty. After a 4-1 defeat home to play-off contenders, Ramsgate, the home dressing room remained locked to all outsiders for over an hour, one can only assume that Alan Devonshire had a lot to say after another sloppy display.

The mark of a good manager is that he can, by force of his own will, change the pattern of a season. The next match was away to Boreham Wood and the opportunity to put bad performances behind them was taken, a brace of goals from Yaku secured a first win since late October. The next thirteen games saw eleven wins, two draws, 29 goals scored, 8 goals conceded and 35 points out of a possible 39. From a dismal 14th place the Beavers had soared to 2nd spot – a 3-2 defeat at Bromley on 3rd March brought the run to an end. However, there was now an air of confidence and a feeling that the team had a chance to do something special.

The defeat at Bromley was followed by a couple of draws and the team slipped back to 5th, but then results picked up again, wins at Tonbridge Angels and Hendon meant that when the Beavers met AFC Wimbledon at Beveree on March 24th they had climbed back to 3rd. The Dons were 2nd and looking good for the Championship. With a large crowd expected, the club officials took the unusual step of segregating the ground. Due to the level of home attendances rarely rising above 400, and the Dons usually having gates in excess of 2,500, the away fans were handed over two thirds

Elliott Godfrey

---

[8] Bartley is one of the forgotten successes at Hampton playing just 25 games before joining Bournemouth then in Football League Two. He went on to play for Burnley, Leyton Orient, Hibernian and is currently paying for Livingstone in the Scottish Premier. Hampton did not receive a transfer fee.

of the ground, whilst home fans were restricted to the South side (the Simpson Stand end) and the Schools Side, as far as the home dugouts, with additional catering and toilet facilities provided for the away fans. It proved a good move as the attendance on the day was 1,802, over four times the usual crowd. Unfazed by the clamour, a 2-0 home win was recorded, Rob Paris and Ian Hodges providing the goals (shortly after Paris had opened the scoring, Wimbledon were reduced to ten men when O'Leary was red carded following a lunging tackle on Bartley).

There were still eight games left, but, despite a heavy away defeat at Chelmsford City (0-4), a tense 1-0 win over Harrow Borough, courtesy of a Glen Harris header – or was it off his shoulder – sealed victory that put the Beavers in the position that it was theirs to lose. All they had to do was win two of the final three games away to Leyton and home to Heybridge Swifts and Slough Town. On the last but one Saturday of the season a 3-0 win was secured at Leyton. Tuesday 24th April came with Heybridge the visitors, a crowd of over 600 turned up hoping to see the Ryman League Championship secured but party poopers Heybridge did not quite follow the script. In fact, it nearly went very wrong.

Chances went begging, shots into the side netting, Ryan Lake had a penalty saved, before Hodges then opened the scoring at the start of the second half - but Heybridge

Stuart Lake puts Hampton 3-2 ahead

quickly equalised. Hodges then departed the game after two yellow cards cranking up the pressure and then Heybridge took the lead. Only a last-minute equaliser by Stuart Lake meant that the championship was still in Hampton's grasp. The last day of the season against already relegated Slough Town meant that either Hampton or Bromley could take the championship (if Hampton lost and Bromley won at Boreham Wood). On a beautiful sunny day 1,055 turned up to watch a see-saw match. Ex-Beaver, Matt Miller gave Slough a 25th minute lead (Bromley were 1-0 up); Hodges headed in an equaliser. Hodges then repeated his earlier feat with another header to put Hampton ahead in the 48th minute before that man, Miller, against the run of play, scored again with 12 minutes remaining for 2-2 (Bromley still winning). A repeat of the final game failure the previous season suddenly looked on the cards.

Finally, Hampton took the game by the scruff of the neck, Stuart Lake drove in an eighteen yarder and Elliott Godfrey struck home a confident penalty to make it, in the end, a comfortable (!) 4-2 win capturing the championship of the Isthmian League for the first time in the club's history. Dean Wells' lucky underpants had clearly done their job!
Cue wild celebrations on the pitch and on the terraces. Champagne flows, balloons fly into the sky, cheers ring out loud. The Chairman had printed up 500 Championship T-Shirts that were distributed to the Hampton faithful as supporters flooded onto the pitch. It was a good job his players delivered on the day or someone was going to get a job lot to sell at Kempton Market!

What would those who in 1921 set out to form a football club called Hampton FC made of it all. In their day, the Isthmian League was the pinnacle of Amateur Football, playing on park football pitches throughout South West Middlesex it would have seemed unimaginable that their bunch of lads from the local village would one day sit at the top of the Isthmian League – I think that they would have been proud and held up a glass (probably beer) to toast the success. Runners-Up, Bromley, won their way through the play-offs and joined the Beavers in promotion to the Conference South.

Fortunately, Cup matches did not cause too much of a distraction to the main aim of winning the championship. The FA Cup saw a penalty shoot-out defeat by Billericay Town. The FA Trophy run was brought to an end at Windsor & Eton (0-2) after a 5-3 thumping of Hitchin Town. The Middlesex Senior Cup saw a quick exit at home to Harrow Borough (0-3), whilst there was a run to the Middlesex Charity Cup Quarter Finals where, with more important matters to deal with, a home defeat to Brook House (1-2) was brushed under the carpet. A first match exit away to Kingstonian in the League Cup (2-3) may have pleased the Ks fans but Hampton had bigger fish to fry. The Beavers did pick up one piece of silverware when they defeated Harrow Borough 2-0 in the Middlesex Super Cup, a match-up between the previous season's winners of the Middlesex Senior and Charity Cups.

The club celebrated the season with a plush dinner and dance at the Richmond Hill Hotel.

Ian Hodges netted 24 goals during the season; Lawrence Yaku scored 17 whilst the elegant Elliott Godfrey notched up 11 goals. The ever consistent, Barrie Matthews appeared in 50 out of 52 games played, Matt Lovett made 49 starts, only missing 3 games, whilst Dean Wells also clocked up 49 even the veteran Lawrence Yaku recorded 45 appearances. Consistency was the watchword for the season. Season 2007/08 offered an unknown; a new adventure, with new places to visit and new opportunities.

Conference South: 2007/08 Season

The Football Conference South – sponsored by Blue Square (an Internet Betting Company) - was to use the old cliché a whole new ball game. Having been used in its entire footballing life to be facing teams either in the local area or perhaps as far afield as Essex, Kent and the Sussex coast, the club now faced some serious travelling. The South division covered, as it implied, the whole of the South of England (and Wales), Newport County, in South Wales; Weston-super-Mare, on the north Somerset coast; up to Cambridge City; Braintree Town in Essex, down to Eastbourne Borough in Sussex and into Hampshire to Havant & Waterlooville. The costs of running the football club would rise as travel costs increased with the occasional use of overnight stays in hotels envisaged. The player budget was increased – but nowhere near most other clubs in the division. There was also the need to think about the cost of possible ground improvements that might be needed to stay at this level. The estimated mileage for Hampton travelling to and from the other teams was 1,327 miles (the lowest being Fisher Athletic with 1,238 and highest Weston-super-Mare, 2992!).

The supporters of Hampton approached the new season with plenty of enthusiasm and a hefty dollop of reality. The majority looking forward to the new opposition and places to visit, perhaps a few weekends away, but fully anticipating it to be a very short stay indeed, a season at most, followed by relegation back to whence they had come. How wrong they were!

During the summer the problem of the missing Boardroom was resolved by Chairman Cole, who managed to source a two-floor structure that would not have looked out of place at a cricket ground or racecourse. Boardroom and Hospitality Suite – in one!

The pre-season had the usual spread of friendlies including a visit from Gateshead. Hampton welcomed back former chairman, Graham Wood, in his guise of 'The Heed's' Chairman; a 1-0 win to the home side with Ian Hodges carrying on where he left off. Alan Devonshire made very few additions to his squad, welcoming back central defender Orlando Jeffery after two seasons away and a youngster, Shaun McAuley, a promising forward, from Hayes.

The first game in the new league was a stern test of Hampton's credentials from an Eastbourne Borough side that had narrowly missed out on the previous season's play-offs. The Sussex club left with all three points thanks to a 2-0 win. To rub salt into the wounds Kelvin McIntosh was sent off and faced an immediate three match ban. Following that baptism of fire, the Beavers settled down and by the end of October were sitting in 5th place, thanks to several good away wins (4-2 at Bognor Regis Town, and 5-0 at Thurrock). On the 1st December, a 5-1 demolition of Weston-super-Mare propelled Hampton up to 3rd place in the table. The Beavers only lost 3 games at home and 4 games away from Beveree, a mark of their consistency.

However, that was largely still all in the future. It is an old adage that the course of true love never runs smooth and so it was with Hampton. In mid-September events occurred that almost derailed the season and also brought into question the entire future of the club. Rumours began circulating that all was not well behind the scenes.

Since September 2005, when David Cole had taken over, the club had been run, in most respects, as an offshoot of his company MEM Retail Marketing Services. Many important day-to-day roles were taken by MEM staff – some part-time, some full-time. In effect MEM ran the club and were involved in all decision making, including financial matters. All, as they say, seemed rosy in the Beveree garden until MEM lost a valuable contract with a major high street retailer and with that any finance was withdrawn. A number of key people resigned from the club over the summer, a sure sign that not everything was quite what it seemed: former Chairman, Bob Hayes, and Company Secretary Nick Hornsey left their posts. Almost immediately a number of outstanding bills came to light including rates, rent, brewery and energy costs – any of which could have brought down the club. Mr Cole was asked to cease involvement with the club on 18th September by the two largest shareholders, Alan Simpson and Graham Wood– almost two years to the day since he took over. MEM shortly thereafter went into administration following a petition by HMRC for unpaid PAYE.

Cole's departure naturally gave rise to concern that Alan Devonshire might follow him out of the club.

"It is fair to say I am considering things at the moment, said Devonshire, *"I have got to work things out in my own mind. It is not my position to comment on what has gone on this week."*

Steve McPherson

Apart from officials to run the football side of things, the club was left with one Director, Chas Milner, a locally based accountant, and, once again, ex-

Chairman Bob Hayes came in to oversee the club. The club was exceedingly lucky that it had a loyal supporter base. A temporary management committee to organise the day to day running was set up under Supporters Club Chairman, Larry Dann, whilst a way forward was sought. As the scale of financial woes became apparent the Supporters Club would morph into the Supporters Trust. The position of Chairman remained vacant until 1st June the following year, however there was a white knight waiting in the wings. Steve McPherson was a successful businessman involved in Insurance Brokerage based in Hampton Hill. He had previously been a player at the club making 11 appearances before moving on to play for Dorking and Egham Town. In the meantime, Club President Alan Simpson agreed to bankroll the club for a month whilst alternative finance was found.

As can happen in real life there was a sense of serendipity as to how McPherson came to be involved in the club – which is worth recounting at this point. He was returning by helicopter from a business engagement when it became apparent that due to a bomb scare, Heathrow Airport was closed. Seeking a place to land McPherson contacted Bob Hayes asking for permission to land on the Beveree pitch.

Chas Milner started a dialogue and Commercial Manager, Mark Kemp, persuaded McPherson to join Milner as a Director in October. McPherson found that the club, financially, was in a bad way but together, with Milner, they worked on a plan to save the club, and engage with the creditors to arrange a system of repaying the various debts. Fortunately, most creditors saw the sense of structured repayments over a negotiated period of time rather having to write off the debts completely. The club did not own the ground, had no real assets apart from a couple of tractors and maybe a few players on contract that could be sold – assuming another club wanted them.

Some creditors requested immediate payment, and those were paid off immediately, by having to make personal contributions, to prevent the club going 'to the wall'.

The actions that McPherson and his colleagues took enabled Hampton to continue to function, leaving Alan Devonshire to concentrate on the football and not on the debt situation. It is worth noting here that Berkhamsted Town Football Club expired during the same season due to an unpaid energy bill, rumoured to have been about £15k, unable to find a saviour to get them out of trouble. Operating at a higher level of football the club was also subject to annual ground inspections by the Football Association – at the end of the season Cambridge City, having failed theirs, was automatically relegated back to the Southern League, despite finishing 14th.

The uncertainty surrounding the club immediately after Cole's departure was felt on the pitch with a flat performance drawing 1-1 against Maidenhead Utd. The hangover didn't last long however, and off field issues were quickly put to one side as the Beavers went on to win seven of their next eight games including three FA Cup wins over Braintree, Worthing and Wealdstone taking them into the First Round Proper for only the second time in their history. It was the furthest Devonshire had gone in the Cup as a manager. The reward was a home tie against League 2 side Dagenham and Redbridge and given their form Hampton fancied their chances. It was also going to be Devonshire's 250th game in charge. Unfortunately, in the run up to the game, the Beavers were dealt a blow with the loss of star striker Lawrence Yaku, who had to attend a family funeral, and Stuart Lake who had picked up a fifth yellow card in the previous round and was now suspended.

2,252 fans turned out to watch the game and Hampton acquitted themselves well dominating much of the first half play which ended goalless. Despite a strong start to the second period, the league side proved more clinical in their finishing and progressed with a 3-0 win which did not truly reflect the balance of the game.

"The boys are distraught," said Devonshire. *"For the first hour, I thought there was only one team in it. We held our own and looked the better team and played the football. We thought it would just be a matter of time before we scored, but we got hit with a sucker punch which hurt us and knocked our confidence. The younger boys will have to learn from this. The target of getting to at least the first round will be the same again next year. I am very proud of the boys. Most of them did themselves justice. Some didn't play as well as I'd have liked, but I thought Elliott Godfrey was the best player on the pitch."*

Orlando Jeffrey comes close with a header cleared off the line. Alan Inns looks on.

The FA Trophy produced a quick exit away at Bishops Stortford in the first round. In the other cup competitions, the Conference experimented with its own league cup, the Setanta Shield, and after wins against Dorchester Town and Newport County, Forest Green Rovers from the Conference National ended interest narrowly winning 1-0 at the Beveree. Better fortune came in the Middlesex Senior Cup, the Beavers victorious for the second time in three seasons, beating Hendon 3-0 at Uxbridge on Easter Monday.

Progress in the League title race remained encouraging as Hampton went undefeated from mid-September through to the middle of February when they finally went down to a 3-0 mid-week defeat at Braintree Town, a side that had won every game against the Beavers since 2001. Hampton still held onto 3rd place behind Lewes and Eastbourne Borough. Two other bogey sides, Fisher Athletic and Bromley where Hampton had not won since 1975, proved more amenable with two victories before Hampton went on to see out the season undefeated. On the way they defeated Champions elect Lewes 6-0 at the Beveree, not enough to change the title outcome but perhaps one of the best performances and most satisfying of the Devonshire era.

Third place was the highest league finish ever by the club and achieved in the very first season in the Conference South, a remarkable feat. It earned the Beavers a play-off place where Hampton took on fourth placed Fisher Athletic in a two-leg semi-final. Second placed Eastbourne took on Braintree Town in the other semi. A 1-1 draw at Fisher was followed by a 0-0 draw at the Beveree, in front of an excellent crowd of 1,489. Neither side could find the vital breakthrough and so the game went into extra time and then penalties. In the penalty shoot-out that followed, the Beavers kept their nerve converting all of their spot kicks including one from 'keeper Matt Lovett which any Hampton forward would have been proud to have scored. Fisher skied two of their three efforts into the Simpson stand to send Hampton into the final.

Hampton were now set to play Eastbourne Borough in a one-off final at a neutral venue, Gravesend & Northfleet, on Thursday, 8th May. Except at very short notice the game was switched to Stevenage Borough (there are stories of supporters of both teams turning up at the wrong ground!). The attendance of 1,077 was disappointing for such a prestigious tie and the change in venue clearly didn't help. The game itself was a very tight affair but with Hampton looking the better of the two sides. Ryan Lake came closest to opening the scoring with a shot tipped onto the post but with defences dominating play the game looked again to heading for extra time until Eastbourne scored twice in the last 5 minutes to leave Hampton crestfallen.

Hampton line up: Matt Lovett; Graham Harper, Ryan Lake (Glenn Harris, 85), Orlando Jeffrey, Stuart Lake, Dean Wells, Alan Inns, Elliott Godfrey (Shaun McAuley,78), Ian Hodges, Lawrence Yaku, Francis Quarm. Subs not used: Rob Paris[9], Marcello Fernandes & Barrie Matthews.

The position of Chairman remained vacant until 1st June when Steve McPherson formally took over the role. He was joined on the board by another ex-footballing businessman, Steve O'Neil.

On 19th April the club were able to announce that Alan Devonshire had signed a new 2 year contract which would run to the end of the 2009/10 season.

Matt Lovett only missed one game out of the 58 played (Kieron Drake, getting a lone outing in goal); Orlando Jeffery, 53 appearances; Elliott Godfrey and Dean Wells each making 51.

---

[9] Rob Paris played twice for Anguilla against El Salvador in a World Cup qualifier in February. They lost 12-0 and 4-0. Rob did not play again for his country.

Lawrence Yaku led the scoring with 23 goals; Elliott Godfrey, 21, Ian Hodges 18 and Shaun McAuley, 13. If Alan Devonshire could keep the bulk of his squad together there was a feeling that this bunch of players could improve and even win the league and send them into the sunlit uplands of the Football Conference.

Conference South: 2008/09 Season

During the summer the club announced that after a three-year absence it was bringing back a Reserve team to compete in the Suburban Football League to be managed by Andy Cook. Also, that the shirt sponsorship had been given to a local charity based in Hampton Hill, 'African Revival', but bigger, by far, was the news that the opening pre-season friendly would be against Premiership's West Ham United. West Ham would be sending their full first team squad to play the Beavers on the evening of 17th July, the day before they would be jetting off to Canada for a pre-season tour. Such was the interest that the game was made all-ticket and on the night an attendance of 3,118 – a new ground record. True their word, the Hammers team on the night was:

Francis Quarm showing off his goal celebration

Rob Green; Lucas Neill, Joe Widdowson, Anton Ferdinand, Callum Devonport, Dean Ashton, Craig Bellamy, Kyel Reid, Mark Noble, Hayden Mullins, Julian Faubert. On the bench was Tony Stokes, Junior Stanislaus, Scott Parker, Carlton Cole, Luis Boa-Morte, Jack Collison, Bonz N'Gala, Jordan Spence, Ashley Miller, Zavon Hines, Jimmy Walker.

Millions of pounds of football talent were on display on a perfect evening for football. The Hammers won 4-2, with Francis Quarm (who worked for West Ham[10]) scoring the opening goal and Lawrence Yaku the Beavers' second. Bellamy (2), Noble and Hines scoring for the illustrious visitors.

Hampton Chairman Steve McPherson was excited at the prospects for the new season and promised that the directors would do everything necessary to support the management by attracting the funds to drive the club forward.

Incoming players to join Devonshire's squad were defenders John Scarborough and Craig Tanner (both from Sutton United), forward Ben Wright (Fleet Town) and midfielder Robbie Kember (Eastbourne Borough). However, two fan favourites, Elliott Godfrey (over 180 appearances and 53 goals) and Alan Inns had left for AFC Wimbledon. Inns was one of the few players who had been at the club at the start of the Devonshire era, whilst nine-year veteran, Dudley Gardner, following a succession of ankle injuries, retired from playing but remained as a member of the management team. Rob Paris moved on to Burnham having had an injury-disrupted end to the previous season. Losing Godfrey was a blow, but Hampton could not compete with the sort of offers being made by Wimbledon. Devonshire commented:

---

[10] At the time Francis worked in West Ham's IT department. His volleyed goal from a corner would not have been out of place at Upton Park.

"There are so many teams throwing around big money this season it is getting silly. My budget hasn't really changed for as long as I have been here, and I'm used to that".

John Scarborough challenges Dean Ashton -photo Dealinepix, HakanYaxici

The Beavers, however, were not particularly quick out of the blocks with a record of two wins, four draws and two defeats in their opening eight games. They were dumped out of the League Cup 3-0 at Braintree but then started to build some momentum with a run of seven consecutive victories, two of which came in the early qualifying rounds of the FA Cup. The Fourth Qualifying Round saw a home draw against Brackley, the first ever meeting between the two sides but the game was over-shadowed by a terrible fire that destroyed the historic Garrick Villa on the Hampton Court Road which blocked off access to Hampton for most of the day. The Brackley players were forced to decamp from their coach at Kempton Park and walk the rest of the way to the Beveree. The incident didn't seem to put them off their stride as they won out with the only goal of the game, a second half header, leaving Hampton's Cup hopes also up in smoke. They fared no better in the FA Trophy going out first time of asking at home to Bury Town.

Leaving cup disappointment behind, Hampton then went on a thirteen-match unbeaten run in the League, picking up 33 points from a possible 39, the run ending with a 1-0 defeat home by Newport County. At the end of November, the Beavers held AFC Wimbledon to a 1-1 draw at Kingsmeadow in front of a 3,366 crowd (Dean Wells getting on the end of a Ben Wright free kick to equalise for the Beavers). The result kept Hampton in 4th place, eight points behind leaders, Chelmsford City, and a point ahead of AFC Wimbledon (who had a game in hand). Unfortunately left back, Craig Tanner, broke his ankle in the game and missed the rest of the season.

Come January, 20 year old Ben Wright, who had scored 13 goals in 26 games, was attracting a lot of attention from league scouts including Roy Hodgson's Fulham. After training with Fulham, Club Chairman Steve McPherson agreed a deal thought to include a record club transfer fee of £50,000 and an announcement made to the press. Wright went for his medical but Hodgson decided to turn down the deal at the last minute, reasons unknown. However, the disappointment was short lived as Peterborough, then riding high in League 1, swooped in to capture Wright.[11] Devonshire recruited Kieran Knight from Hayes & Yeading to fill the gap left by Wright's departure.

In any other season Hampton's strong run might have seen them top the division but Wimbledon were equally relentless. Towards the end of February, Hampton were in second place, but it was a case of thus far but no further.

---

[11] Wright made only five appearances for Peterborough and later re-joined Alan Devonshire for a spell at Braintree Town. Much of his career has been spent around the upper reaches of non-league football but alas never quite made the grade at pro level.

Whether the loss of Wright contributed to Hampton's failure to clinch top spot is debatable. Wimbledon already had a much better goal difference. By now, it was AFC Wimbledon who were leading the way, Hampton seven points adrift – but with a game in hand. In early March Newport County were the visitors with Hampton looking to equal the league record of 10 straight victories and close the gap. Alas they suffered a second defeat of the season to the South Wales side and the record went begging. Another unexpected defeat, 4-0 away at Welling Utd gave Wimbledon a nine point lead but then they started to falter themselves when Welling inflicted a home defeat that enabled Hampton to close the gap once again. The Beavers pulled within three points of the top spot with a game in hand (although considerably worse goal difference) but then lost 3-2 away at Chelmsford who were also pushing for a play-off place. Whilst mathematically there was still a chance of overhauling Wimbledon

Stuart Lake celebrates scoring against Eastleigh – photo Jeff Beasley

much was going to depend on the return league fixture in the penultimate game of the season.

Off the field Hampton also found itself having to rapidly upgrade facilities to meet new regulations for joining the Conference National should they win promotion. This included extra seating capacity which was added by the purchase of a somewhat derelict temporary stand from Barnet. The stand was erected on a newly laid concrete base at the far end of the ground the cost of the works running into several thousands of pounds. This unbudgeted cost was to have consequences in later seasons.

With the visit of AFC Wimbledon on Saturday 18th April another big crowd expected, and a second all-ticket game was called for. The ground record was broken again, this time 3,225 squeezed into the compact Beveree. Once again, it was the visiting fans that were given the majority of the ground and they were syphoned in from the meadow and entering at the halfway line. The majority of the ground was a sea of blue and yellow making it feel very much like a home game for the Wombles.

Hampton needed to win. The match started slowly but soon developed into a titanic struggle. Shortly after half time Hampton got the break they wanted. A quick clearance from Matt Lovett found its way to Francis Quarm who slotted home from the edge of the six-yard area. Hampton now needed to hold on to the vital three points. Time ticked by but with just eight minutes to go AFC got a stroke of luck. John Scarborough rushing to clear the ball collided with Marcello Fernandes and went down heavily with a serious injury to his leg. With the ball out of play and two Hampton defenders prostrate on the ground, Referee Tony Mason inexplicably waved play on. Wimbledon took the throw-in, and the resulting cross was headed home by Jon Main, who Scarborough would have been marking had he have not been injured. Scarborough was then stretchered off with a badly gashed thigh. Bad sportsmanship by AFC, the referee overcome by the occasion or a case of Hampton switching off ?– you decide. Mr Main refused to speak to an understandably angry Alan Devonshire after the game. The draw was enough for the visitors but the manner in which it was earned left a bad taste.

AFC Wimbledon secured promotion whilst, for the second season running, Hampton had to go through the lottery of the play-offs having finished a record breaking 2nd. They were paired off with 4th placed Chelmsford City, who had spoilt Hampton's promotion chances just weeks earlier, for a two-leg semi-final. The contest was virtually over in the first leg at Chelmsford as Hampton exacted revenge with a 3-1 win with goals from Lawrence Yaku 2 and Ian Hodges – Hodges then blotted his copybook by being sent off for two cautions! Eastleigh who had finished third took a 4-2 advantage into their second leg against Hayes & Yeading.

The second leg at the Beveree was a dull 0-0 draw, which saw the Beavers through to another final, not against Eastleigh as expected but Hayes & Yeading who had turned the tables with a 4-0 second leg comeback. Ominously Hampton had failed to beat Hayes & Yeading in the league season, drawing 0-0 away and losing 2-3 at home way back in August.

The Conference changed their rules for this season and decreed that the Play Off Final must be played at the home of the highest-placed club, which therefore meant that Hampton would host Hayes & Yeading United five days later on Thursday 7th May. Due to the shortage of time between the two games – and bearing in mind that there was also a Bank Holiday on the Monday, the club decided that there was insufficient time to make the game all-ticket. Neither club had massive support so it was reasonable to assume that a crowd in the vicinity of 1,500 would turn up. How wrong everyone was. When the gates were closed there were 3,111 inside – okay, maybe there were a few more, however, outside Beveree were upwards of 500 queuing up Station Road who could not get into the ground!

Of Hampton's play-off Final squad, 11 players had appeared in the previous play-off final against Eastbourne. This time Ryan Lake and Lawrence Yaku were on the subs bench and McAuley promoted to a starting role. Knight and Kember were the only two new faces starting. It was a testament to the consistency that Devonshire had built in the squad.

Team: Lovett, Harper, Fernandes, Jeffrey, McAuley, Wells ©, S Lake, Quarm, Hodges, Knight, Kember. Subs: Yaku, Tyson, Badu, Scarborough, R Lake.

On a warm and dry evening another fascinating contest ensued in which first one side and then the other seemed to have won the game. Hayes took an early 7th minute lead and pressed Hampton throughout the half. Hampton were showing the greater nerves and couldn't find a goal before the halftime break arrived.

Then early in the second half, a lobbed pass from Quarm found McAuley in space in the right-hand channel and his low angled shot squirmed under the Hayes keeper, Delroy Preddie, and just over the line for 1-1. A bit of good fortune but it was the lifeline Hampton needed. With just 20 minutes to go the Beavers took a 2-1 lead through Ian Hodges with one of the most remarkable goals ever seen at the Beveree. Preddie who had a habit of kicking from the floor, failed to realise that Hodges was lurking behind him as he prepared to clear up field. Hodges, his head bandaged Terry Butcher-style, suddenly appeared from nowhere like a pantomime villain – in fact the whole ground could see him apart from Preddie – and despite the shouts of "behind you!" from the Hayes supporters, Hodges nipped in to score the cheekiest of goals to grace a major final.

But Hampton's lead and Preddie's embarrassment lasted just three minutes as midfielder Steven Gregory scored a quick-fire reply – his cross cum shot seemed to catch the breeze, floated over Lovett and in off the far post. Moments later and the game was turned on its head as Fitzgerald's shot from the edge of the box went under Lovett and into the net for 3-2. It was tough on Lovett so often Hampton's saviour and to top off the evening Lovett was sent off in the last minute after scything down his nemesis Fitzgerald near the dugouts as Hayes & Yeading broke clear from a Hampton corner, the entire team committed forward. It completed a miserable evening for him and the Beavers. Four errors by two of the league's best keepers showed the tension of the game. Coach Dudley Gardner had some consoling words for Lovett:

"Both goalkeepers made mistakes and people remember those more than anything. Matt has been superb all season and is in no way to blame for it. Most of the players froze on the night. The expectations were a little bit higher because we were at home, but we really thought we could do it. In the end it didn't happen for us and only three or four performed as you'd expect, and they were the better side."

Once again, as the massive crowd filed out after the game, the Beavers were left disappointingly short of their target of a place at the highest level of the Non-League game. Alan Devonshire would go into his seventh season in charge trying to get the Beavers over the hump that was the play-offs.

For the record, Matt Lovett topped the appearances table with 49 closely followed by Dean Wells on 47 and John Scarborough on 43. Despite finishing 2nd Hampton's only two marksmen to get into double figures were Lawrence Yaku on 18 and Ben Wright on 13, followed by Ian Hodges on 9.

Conference South: 2009/10 Season

So, could Hampton, and Alan Devonshire in particular rouse his troops one more time to build on the successes of the recent season? Step by step the club had continued to improve its position in the Football Pyramid, could this seemingly unstoppable progress be maintained to produce the ultimate, promotion to the upper echelons of the Football Conference?

During the summer Brian Barwick[12] joined the club board as a director. Mr Barwick had years of experience as a media executive at the BBC and ITV and at the Football Association where he was Chief Executive until 2008 appointing Fabio Capello as England manager. It was hoped that Barwick could use his football connections to drive the club forward.

"I'm pretty well connected in football and in the commercial world," said Barwick to the local press. *"I think it is inconceivable that I wouldn't be of some use. We've got to give Dev every opportunity to get as strong a squad as he can and get as many people to watch us as we can. What Alan has done is quite remarkable. Our job is to support him and make sure he gets the right opportunities to keep the momentum going."*

Marc Cranfield- Adams, a former Mayor of Richmond Upon Thames also joined as a non-executive director. On the administrative side the club were looking for a new Press Officer following Les Rance stepping down after many years of service; also, a new Club Shop had been installed in the inner car park. The pitch had been worked on during the close season to provide an excellent playing surface.

The South division had been joined by promoted sides Dover Athletic and old rivals Staines Town, and by relegated Lewes, Woking and Weymouth from the National division. Lewes had lasted only one season in the National League and perhaps showed for Hampton the magnitude of the challenge for a small club to survive in a league now populated by a number of full time ex League sides. Lewes just managed to survive in the Conference South, whilst Weymouth went straight through the division for a double relegation having gone into administration during the season. The financial burden of Conference National was hard for traditional non-league sides to bear with higher playing costs and the need to constantly upgrade facilities. Teams a lot larger than Hampton had been badly burned by the experience of living the dream.

The majority of the previous season's squad remained though the Lake 'brotherhood' was broken up as Ryan, brother of Stuart Lake, left to join Kingstonian, his appearances limited by the form of Craig Tanner now returned from injury. Shaun McAuley also departed tempted away by Eastleigh.

Locally born, Dean Inman made the step up from the Reserves to make a defensive contribution to the team. By the time that the season was up and running further players had been added: Jamie Collins a big name signing from Havant & Waterlooville; Ashley Smith from Maidenhead United; striker Dave Tarpey from Basingstoke Town; keeper Kevin Davies (as cover for Matt Lovett), Craig Dundas from Sutton United (a proven striker) and Michael Lee-Charles, a

---

[12] Brian Barwick OBE was later appointed Chairman of the National League in 2015, leaving under something of a cloud in 2021 after the chaotic suspension of the NL North and South under the impact of Covid. He remained a director at Hampton for only one season.

young striker from Farnborough. At the end of September Nathan Collier joined from Sevenoaks Town, a versatile player who could fulfil roles in defence or in midfield or occasionally as we shall see, attack. Of these new signings only Tarpey and Collier would still be with the club the following season.

During the close season the club entered negotiations to grant a two year extension on Alan Devonshire's contract. However, Cambridge United, then in the Conference National, had asked permission to speak to Devonshire for their vacant managerial role. Chairman Steve McPherson initially turned down the approach but after a two-hour long meeting with Devonshire agreed to let him consider the offer. Thankfully, Devonshire decided to sign his extension, but he had clear ambitions to manage at a higher level.

The versatile Nathan Collier

"Obviously I'm delighted to sign a new contract, I've really enjoyed my time here so far and the success we have enjoyed," Devonshire said. "I'm looking forward to progressing the club over the next couple of years and taking us to even greater achievements. "

A slow start seemed habitual for the Beavers, but Devonshire's experience usually saw his sides gain momentum through the season as others fell by the wayside when pitches got heavier, and the winter nights drew in. Hampton faced something of an injury crisis as the season opened and were missing 'keeper Lovett due to the four game suspension hanging over from the Hayes play-off game. Davies and Chico Ramos deputised for the first four matches. It was a tricky fixture list with early games against two of the more fancied sides, Woking and Newport County – both games were lost.

After ten games the team were in 14th place, having managed only three wins during that period. A case of 'after the Lord Mayors Show', indeed.

Jamie Collins of whom great things were expected did not settle in the side and left after just nine appearances – to rivals Newport County. And that after leaving Havant due to the difficulties of travelling from his Hertfordshire home! But it was a sound decision. He would gain promotion with them.

There were occasional flashes of the previous season's successes – a 4-1 win over Maidenhead United at the end of October, with Ian Hodges scoring a hat-trick. However, there were too many defeats, ofttimes two or three in a row, something which had not been seen for a year or two. A sign of players ageing together or possibly a lack of investment? The momentum simply did not materialise.

Devonshire knew that he had to find cover for Lawrence Yaku who was now pushing veteran status and could not be relied on to play the full 90 minutes in every game. Lee-Charles and Tarpey were the next generation but were much less experienced. Tarpey was sent out on loan to Walton & Hersham to get more game time and eventually came back to deliver some goals which saw him equal top goal scorer with Craig Dundas, both with 10 goals. The main burden fell on Hodges and Dundas but they both suffered injury prone seasons. Francis Quarm and John Scarborough also picked up long-term injuries and this certainly had something to do with the disappointing results. At one stage the club was languishing in 19th place (6th February) five points ahead of Lewes in 20th, but with a precious three games in hand due a run of weather-related postponements.

Around this time the club launched its own Football Academy in conjunction with St Pauls School, Sunbury, offering 2-year courses, split between education and sport. The Academy would, next season, compete in Conference Youth League, playing matches on a Wednesday afternoon.

Meanwhile, the team remained in and around 18th place until a late rally of four wins in five games moved them up to 14th, a last game home defeat to Lewes being of no consequence. At no point in the season had the side reached higher than 9th place and most of the time languished in the bottom half, such a contrast to the previous two seasons.

The underlying issue was that finances were constrained after the exertions of the previous season and the early Cup exits which led to the trimming of the budgets. The impact of the global financial meltdown that hit the economy at the end of 2008 led to everyone having to tighten their belts. The club could not afford to invest in the quality of players needed to refresh the squad and budget cuts saw the squad trimmed. Fan favourites Marcello Fernandes, Graham Harper, Jon McDonald and Francis Quarm all left the club. Quarm had played the first seven games but then picked up a knee injury that required surgery.

First team assistant manager Dudley Gardner interviewed at the end of January was candid about the reality of the situation:

"Our budget is now equivalent of a good Combined Counties Premier League side. A team in the bottom half of the Ryman League Premier Division will have bigger budgets," he said. *"Staying up in those circumstances would be a great achievement - the equivalent of getting promoted. The chairman and supporters club has put a lot of money and effort into the club, but the economic climate and the cancelled games have taken their toll. We'd love to change things, but there is no money there to do it. We've just got to keep our heads up and get on with it. Dev is a winner and we'll be giving our all to do it."*

Newer recruits such as Dean Inman, Dave Tarpey, Nathan Collier and James Simmonds were all to go on to decent non-league careers but at this stage their lack of experience was unable to plug the gaps left by injuries and departures. What recruitment there was came from the lower leagues.

Hodges, who had been struggling all season to recapture his form after a hernia operation, and Yaku were unable to repeat their goalscoring feats and goals dried up from midfield.

In the F A Cup a run as far as the 4th Qualifying Round saw an exit at the hands of Sutton United (though Dundas did manage to score a goal against his former teammates). The FA Trophy saw an exit at the 1st Round stage at Lewes, after a replay.

Matt Lovett in action

Out of a possible 51 games, Craig Dundas led the way with 49 appearances; Lawrence Yaku, 48 games (though 13 were off the subs bench; Barrie Matthews with 47; Matt Lovett and Orlando Jeffrey, made 46 each. In terms of goalscoring Dundas and Tarpey were the only ones to get into double figures with 10 each, a lack of scoring power giving a clue to the drop in league placings.

There was one bright spark and that was provided by the reserves who won the Suburban League (North) Championship under the guidance of former player Mark Harper. In the following season Harper became first team coach whilst Andy Smith took over the Reserves.

Conference South: 2010/11 Season

New season, new hopes, new players and a not a few departures as budget cuts bit hard. Devonshire spoke to the local press:

"We have got to rebuild, and it is probably going to be one of the toughest jobs I've had."

Amongst those leaving were player of the season Craig Dundas (back to Sutton United after a one-season stay), and Stuart Lake to Basingstoke Town after four years. John Scarborough left to join Bromley. In all 15 regulars had left the club over the previous 15 months due to financial constraints. At board level Brian Barwick resigned having made little impact on the club.

Craig Tanner

Devonshire seemed to be keeping a brave face on things. New blood coming in included midfielder, Jamie Simmonds, returning from a stint in Spain at Glenn Hoddle's Football Academy, and forward Charlie Moone, from much closer to home, Woking. Other new faces were Danny Allen Page, a right back from Hayes & Yeading, Dave Stephens a centre half from Uxbridge, Lloyd Boateng another central defender from Fisher Athletic, and Ryan Adams from Walton & Hersham. Also new was a yellow away kit, not a colour previously associated with the Beavers.

Devonshire was more hopeful that Ian Hodges would return to form after a difficult previous season, and he scored in the pre-season friendly against a QPR XI. However, a hamstring injury in the second league game led to him relegated back to the periphery for a number of matches and his goalscoring contribution never really materialised. That duty fell largely to Tarpey and Moone although neither made double figures for the season; Lawrence Yaku was the only player to achieve that target.

Again, it was a modest start to the league programme with just one win and four draws in the first six games. However, a couple of wins over Bishops Stortford and high-flying Dover Athletic left Hampton in a comfortable 6th place after ten games, just one place outside the play-off spots. There was a degree of optimism that the young squad would not struggle as had been feared.

If the 4-0 win in the FA Cup against Romford suggested that things were moving nicely on course, the next round saw the Beavers crash and burn away at Isthmian League Harrow Borough, 2-1. The lack of consistency was frustrating but with a thin squad, a number of injuries and suspensions,

Devonshire's options to refresh the side were limited. As the autumn progressed, form began to fall away, and Hampton started to drift away from upper reaches of the league. To make matters worse 'keeper Matt Lovett suffered a cruciate knee injury in the league game against Woking and it was feared that reconstructive surgery would put him out of the game for up to 9 months. Joe Talbot came in to take over the gloves but then himself got injured meaning Reserve Team keeper Adam Carpenter had to step in. In the end Lovett decided not to undergo surgery and returned to the team in the New Year.

The only competition where any run was put together came in the FA Trophy where Hampton won through to the 2nd Round and an away draw at Graham Wood's Gateshead. That game was pushed into January due to bad weather causing widespread postponements across the country. In fact, Hampton went without a league game for the whole of December and then had to play catch-up.

The long trip to the North East was not a happy one as Hampton were soundly thrashed 6-0, outclassed by the full-time side. In a very one sided first half, Hampton held out until the 37th minute until a headed goal from a corner put the hosts 1-0 up. Hampton survived until half time a but a couple of goals early in the second period killed off the

Alan Devonshire

tie as a competition. Three more goals rained in in the last 15 minutes as the Hampton players tired. Carpenter was given Man of the Match suggesting the score line could have been much greater. It was Hampton's heaviest defeat for some seasons. Shortly after Dave Stephens quit the club for Braintree Town who were league leaders, a case of if you can't beat them, join them.

In November, the club announced an ambitious new five-year business plan to raise funds for redevelopment of the Old Stand, new changing and hospitality facilities and an all-weather training pitch on the top field. An expansion of the Academy was also proposed. The plan, however, was strong on ideas but lacking in execution and was quietly forgotten. It was difficult enough to keep the day to day funding going let alone start a major new investment initiative.

Off the field, things seemed to reflect the less than happy fortunes on the pitch. A break in on New Year's Day was followed by a power cut 30 minutes before the kick-off against Chelmsford City leaving the large crowd having to turn around and head home. The lack of home games was crippling the cashflow.

Hampton still had to play 22 league games in 3 months, and it was now turning into a battle to avoid relegation rather than the hoped for play off place. The Beavers had drifted down to 18th place just two places above the three relegation spots with just five league wins all season. Creating and scoring goals was at the heart of the problem.

Some old faces were drafted in to try and steady the ship: Francis Quarm, John Scarborough, Jamie Collins and Graham Harper all returned to the squad and Ian Hodges got a run of starting appearances albeit not scoring many goals. Midfielder Paul Johnson was recruited from Carshalton and Liam Stone, another goalkeeper from Badshot Lea. Some youngsters from the Youth and Reserve sides were blooded, Dan Thompson, Billy Witham and Gustavo Sousa Mota but none forced their way into the side on a permanent basis. With the subs bench heavily populated with Reserves and Youth Team players, the financial position was clear for all to see. The changes did little to alter overall results and Hampton remained uncomfortably in the lower reaches of the league though never dropping into one of the three relegation places.

The final weeks of the season saw just one more win and a run of eight games in which only three goals were scored. The final four games all saw defeats, but Hampton survived in 18th place, a miserable end to a largely miserable season. From 42 games they managed 42 points. 43 goals scored was the third lowest in the division, only relegated Lewes and St Albans City fared worse. Braintree Town went up as Champions and were joined in the Conference National by Ebbsfleet Utd via the play offs. With the prospect of another financially challenged season to come, there was justifiable speculation whether Alan Devonshire would see out his contract.

Dave Tarpey made 46 appearances (including 19 from the bench), out of 51 matches played; Dean Inman, 45 (all starts) and Lawrence Yaku 41 (21 from the bench). Only Yaku managed to score double figures in the League – just – with 10, Moone with 8 and Tarpey with 7, showed the scale of the problem.

It was perhaps no surprise then that Devonshire was open to approaches from other clubs having previously flirted with Cambridge Utd. At the end of season awards in May Steve McPherson announced that Devonshire had taken the manager's job at

Braintree Town, who had just won the Conference South title, following the departure of Rod Stringer who had fallen out with the club over terms.

The Devonshire Effect

Alan Devonshire was in charge of Hampton for just under eight years. In that time from 444 matches, 221 were won; a proud track record, including:

- Promotion from Isthmian Division One (South)
- Isthmian League Play-Off Finalists
- Championship of the Isthmian League
- 3rd place in the Football Conference South
- Runners-up in the Football Conference South
- Football Conference South Play-Off Finalists twice
- 1st Round of the F A Cup
- Middlesex Senior Cup Winners Twice
- Middlesex Senior Cup Runners-up
- Isthmian League Cup Finalists

By any measure, this was the most successful period in the club's history until the arrival of Alan Dowson five years later. Devonshire's long history in the professional game made him a good judge of players and with the right budget he was capable of building winning sides based on the sound principles of defensive solidity and a strong central spine. Some commentators were surprised that his sides didn't play a more expansive passing game given his West Ham "Academy" background. In Ben Wright and Elliot Godfrey, Hampton did possess flair players but there was a healthy degree of pragmatism necessary for the physical demands of the non-league arena. He played to his team's strengths and it hard to say it didn't bring results. Financial constraints clouded the final two seasons at the club, and it is fair to say Hampton could no longer meet his ambition to progress. What would have happened if promotion to the Conference National had been achieved is an interesting question. His subsequent career managing Braintree Town and Maidenhead Utd has been largely spent in the top Conference division and he has tended to stay loyal to his owners having only ever managed three sides in senior football. Perhaps uniquely for any football manager at this level he has never been sacked from a post.

2003-11 Manager's Record

Alan DEVONSHIRE	P	W	D	L	F	A	Pts	Ave Pts	Win %
Combined	444	221	91	132	719	544			49.8
League	340	164	80	96	556	418	572	1.68	48.2
Play Offs	8	3	2	3	7	11			
Cup	96	54	9	33	156	115			

The Supporters' Trust

If you find your club with a Supporters Trust it is usually sign that not all is well or that some crisis has occurred where the :ure of the club has been thrown into doubt. Hampton was no different. When established in 2008, the Beavers Trust was one of the smallest supporters' trusts in the country to be set up and had it not been for the gift of a substantial number of shares by the former Chairman, Graham Wood, the trust would never have got off the ground. Over the years, after some grudging acceptance, the Trust has gone on to play a vital role at the club and one that the Trust and its members can be justifiably proud.

Interestingly the first mention of a supporters' trust had arisen after the departure of Vic Searle as Chairman in 2002 as a means of allowing supporters to invest personally in the club. Moves had been afoot for some time to convert the club into a limited company but never progressed. A supporters' club did exist as a means of general fundraising but had no formal role at the club and without a vehicle to invest in a supporters' trust had to remain just an interesting concept.

Hampton FC had originally been set up as a member's club, an unincorporated body where membership entitled you to one person one vote, but each member had full personal liability. Active encouragement to become a member was rare, not actively discouraged but equally not something that was promoted. When Graham Wood first became Chairman in 2003, he acted as the catalyst to push forward the incorporation as a condition of him investing and becoming Chairman. Under the proposal all members were given 10 shares in the new company in return for agreeing the new set up.

The major investors in the club such as Graham Wood and Alan Simpson and later Steve McPherson, built up larger shareholdings over the years although the new limited company articles placed a limitation on any one person holding more than 29.9% of the overall shareholding, a precaution built in to prevent the club being controlled by any one individual.

When Graham Wood decided to move back to the North East at the end of the 2005 season to take over as Chairman of his hometown club, Gateshead FC, he retained his shareholding in Hampton but under league rules was not allowed to have any further involvement and resigned as a director. Club Patron Bob Hayes had introduced local businessman David Cole to the club as a potential new sponsor and investor and substantial new investment was made into both the playing staff and facilities at the club. Cole was appointed Chairman at the start of the 2005/06 season. Outwardly to supporters this was a continuation of the success started when Wood had taken over as Chairman, with Hampton winning the Isthmian League title in 2007. However, what was less well known was that Cole held no official role at the club other than as sponsor as he was prevented from becoming a director due to an earlier disqualification relating to the failure of one of his previous companies.

The Club had not been aware of this fact until it had been pointed out by the club's bankers. The local press announced that Cole was hoping to seek agreement to carry on as a director of the club, but this was not forthcoming nor indeed likely under the league's "fit and proper person test," and so he was obliged to resign. Cole was still referred to as Chairman in the local press and acted to all intents and purposes as if he was Chairman, but this was not the case. Not that many supporters would have been overly concerned about Company Law issues given the obvious success on the pitch.

With the club on a high following promotion to the Conference South in 2007, there was little inkling that the Club would be plunged into crisis within weeks. However, at the beginning of the new season rumours began to circulate that Cole's latest business venture was in trouble and the flow of funding to the club quickly dried up. Bills went unpaid and staff, who were funded directly from his company were laid off. With large sums owing to HMRC, Cole's business was compulsorily wound up leaving the remaining club directors to find new investors. In due course that investment was found from Steve McPherson and his associates and the immediate crisis abated.

As the main shareholder in Gateshead, Graham Wood was obliged to give up his shareholding in Hampton and offered the shares at token cost to supporters as a means of getting more fan involvement into the club. The existing Supporters Club was keen to pursue the idea and so negotiations were opened in the autumn of 2007 with Supporters Direct to explore whether a Supporters' Trust was a viable project. Wood's shareholding was just over 20% and this represented a more than usually large percentage for a supporters' trust just starting out compared to other trusts at bigger clubs than Hampton. Supporters Direct were prepared to support the idea and after a number of meetings to galvanise support, the new Beavers Trust came into being in April 2008. Larry Dann was appointed as its first Chairman and over 200 supporters signed up as shareholder members.

The Trust was incorporated as an Industrial and Providential Society, a not-for-profit entity, then the favoured model of Supporters Direct who provided guidance and encouragement in the formation of the new entity. The rules of the Trust gave its shareholders one share in return for a minimal annual subscription of £1 with no member able to hold more than one share. In many ways it was back to the model of the old club model but with limited liability protection.

Whilst there was some initial suspicion about the Trust's intentions, it gradually built a good relationship with the club board assisting with a number of projects financially and promoting the club within the wider community. From the outset it was a firm policy not to fund the day to day costs of the club such as player wages but to invest in longer term assets that would otherwise have been a cost to the club thus allowing directors to channel funds elsewhere if required. One of the first major purchases was a club minibus but the variety of purchases ranged from cookers and washing machines to installing irrigation bore holes, a tractor for pitch maintenance, mowers, irrigation pumps, floodlights and a contribution to terrace crush barriers and stand refurbishment. Indeed, the application for the Football Foundation grant to assist with this project was handled by Trust volunteers.

For a number of years, the Trust ran "beat the goalie" competitions at local fairs and ran kids coaching sessions to promote the club. Latterly the Trust has also run a new food bank scheme in conjunction with local charities and businesses, further tying the club into the community and enhancing its credentials as a community focused club.

It was also a policy to ensure that the Trust could continue to invest in shares to maintain its shareholding position so many of the injections of capital were directly linked to further share purchases. One area it did take over day to day costs was the running of the match day programme which had run a up debt with its printers and was running at a regular loss. By tightening controls this debt was gradually paid back and profits made through cultivating local advertisers which had been hitherto neglected.

Not everyone saw the distinction between capital and revenue projects, but it was all too easy for the club to use money donated for expenditure without any real accountability of how that money was spent. In time the club directors came round to a more positive view of the Trust and agreed that two representatives should be invited onto the board with Tony Nash and Larry Dann being the first appointees followed later on by Phil Weller. Representation at board level is through the Trust becoming a corporate director of the club with two nominees representing the Trust's shareholding.

This undoubtedly helped with a better understanding between the parties and led to significant investment being provided over the next few years. And when it came to finding new investors it was the Trust that helped broker the return of Graham Wood and Jacques Le Bars which enabled the club to maintain its forward momentum.

A football club is never short of the need for more and more money. Expectations are that football clubs even at non-league level are run at or near the same standards as professional sides. Ground grading requirements have become ever more stringent with clubs with modest home attendances expected to maintain the same standards as teams with home gates in the thousands. Building reserves to meet these demands is far from easy when supporters would often prefer the recruitment of a star centre forward rather than a new toilet block. Short termism dominates most sports but the old adage "act in haste, repent at leisure," was never more relevant in the non-league world. The Trust's purpose was to take that longer term view and make sure it remains represented at board level.

Undoubtedly without the support of Graham Wood, the Trust could never have got off the ground. It was never the aim to take over the club (not that it could) but was always to work with whoever was chairman or the main investors to ensure that the club was run on a long term sustainable basis. As we move into the third decade of the 21st Century the club faces new challenges never even thought possible just a few months ago and the Supporters Trust movement will need to adapt and ensure that fan engagement remains at the top of their agenda if the club is to continue to thrive.

The Austerity Years 2011-14

Conference South: 2011/2012 Season

Despite interest from outside the club, Chairman Steve McPherson was quick to appoint Devonshire's assistant Mark Harper to the top job. Harper had a distinguished playing career having played for Hampton 61 times in the early 1990s before moving to Kingstonian, Sutton Utd, Farnborough and Aldershot Town. As Hampton's Reserve Team manager, he had achieved title winning success before becoming Assistant to Devonshire.

"I am confident," said McPherson, "that Mark will utilise his vast playing experience of non-league football to ensure that our club will be in safe hands; he is Hampton through and through and also understands the challenges that we face as a Blue Square Conference South club."

The budget was increased slightly giving some room for optimism:

"I think we will have quite a good season and I think we will hold our own."

Harper appointed Andy Smith as his own No2, with Paul Barry, ex-manager of Camberley Town, coming into head up the Reserves. Hopes were for a more attractive style of play compared to the previous seasons although

Mark Harper

budget constraints were such that Harper would need to rebuild the squad. Survival in the league would be his main objective.

"I want to build a lasting football legacy with both the playing and management staff that will sustain this club for many years to come," he said.

"As a club, we recognise the need to adapt and change. The board has given us a realistic budget for the forthcoming season, and we will work within it. I want to find the right balance between spending money on players and investing in coaching and development. We need to seek the best value for the club."

" Experience is critical but our future depends on the younger players coming through the academy system," he said.

James Simmonds

Pre-season friendlies were the usual mix of high-profile games against league sides where Hampton despite defeats showed some promise of a more attractive style of play. Of the previous season's squad, most departed to pastures new. Harper was able to retain Charlie Moone, Dave Tarpey, Nathan Collier, James Simmonds, Paul Johnson and Dean Inman but keeper Matt Lovett remained troubled by the knee injury incurred the previous season. Dean Wells joined Staines Town before joining up again with Alan Devonshire at Braintree Town[13]. Barrie Matthews, often an unsung hero of the Devonshire years, moved to St Albans City.

New faces included central defenders Matt Ruby from Kingstonian and Billy Jeffreys from Ashford Town (Middx), goalkeeper Rodney Chiweshe from Godalming Town, striker Jacob Erskine from Bromley, midfielders Aaron Morgan and right back Lewis Farrell from Hayes and Yeading. In the first game of the season at home to Bromley, only three players from the previous season took the field, Hampton unlucky to lose 2-1 after some controversial refereeing.

However, despite some initial optimism, the first ten league games were to prove challenging for Harper and his new squad. Just two points were picked up before the first win of the season came at home, 3-1 against 5th placed Weston-super-Mare at the end of September. The team showed themselves to be brittle in defence, easily overrun in midfield and prone to conceding soft goals which undermined any good passages of play that the side were capable of showing. Scoring goals remained a problem. Added to this was the propensity to concede penalties and get players dismissed at key moments. A case in point was the away game at Salisbury City where Moone converted an early penalty which gave Hampton the confidence to put in one of their better performances and take the 1-0 advantage through to half time. Within minutes of the restart Hampton were behind and looked like conceding from every opposition attack. Matt Ruby then brought them level with a header only to see Dean Inman sent off and the game lost tamely 4-2. Harper was criticised by fans for tinkering with the line-up and formations, but patchy form of individual players and injuries did not help achieve consistency. Inman and young

---

[13] Despite serving a brief prison sentence at the end of the 2011 season, Wells went on to play league football for Stevenage Borough making his debut in 2014. His cousin George Wells later played for Hampton.

forward Dan Thompson were regularly away on trials at pro clubs with Thompson finally signing for Portsmouth although he had failed to score any goals for Hampton.

Having secured the first win, Harper made a couple of changes for the visit to Arlesey Town in the FA Cup 2nd Qualifying Round. Arlesey like Hampton were struggling badly in the Southern League Premier Division with just two wins all season. The game turned into something of a nightmare for Hampton, conceding a goal in the first minute, and despite equalising through Dave Tarpey, the Beavers went on to concede five times in 25 minutes either side of half time eventually going down 6-2, their heaviest ever FA Cup defeat. The pressure was mounting on Harper, out of the Cup at the first attempt and languishing at the bottom of the league.

The Cup exit was followed by two further league defeats against Tonbridge Angels and Boreham Wood. The Tonbridge game saw the return of Matt Lovett in goal, but he could do nothing to stop a 90th minute penalty denying the Beavers a vital point. Twelve league games in, Hampton were rooted to last place with just six points. Striker Charlie Moone was placed on the transfer list despite being equal top scorer. Erskine was to follow and left the club shortly afterwards. Matt Lovett lasted only three games before recurring injury saw him replaced first by Rodney Chiweshe and then by Craig Ross from Welling Utd. Lovett then broke his leg in a Reserve team match which ended his already troubled season.

Further squad changes were inevitable as Harper tried to find a winning formula and slowly fortunes began to change for the better during the autumn. Loanees Joel Ledgister, a forward from Sutton Utd and JJ O'Donnell, a left back on loan from Luton Town helped improve the squad as did the signings of midfielders Josh Huggins from Didcot Town and Karle Andrews. And then news that there could be a return for Hampton favourite, Darren Powell gave fans real hope that the defensive frailty would finally be addressed. Powell had been released from his last club MK Dons in 2010 and was admittedly a little ring rusty but it was felt that his experience would help galvanise the team. 35 years old Powell had left Hampton for Brentford after helping them to promotion to the Isthmian Premier in 1998, before moving to Crystal Palace, Southampton, Derby County and MK Dons, playing over 250 league games. But his impact was not as immediate as was hoped.

Dave Tarpey

Something of a run was put together in the FA Trophy beating Canvey Island, Conference National side Hayes and Yeading and East Thurrock after a replay giving Hampton an away draw with Northwich Victoria from the Northern Premier league.

Away form proved to be better with league wins picked up at fellow strugglers Maidenhead Utd, Staines Town and Bromley so there was some optimism that Hampton could go further in the Trophy against Northwich Victoria, another side having a difficult season after having been thrown out of their home ground the month before and having lost their entire management team.

However, the game started badly with Hampton conceding in the 4th minute and then losing captain Matt Ruby moments later with what turned out to be a season-ending injury. It finished 4-1; Hampton were never in the game. Even the presence of Darren Powell couldn't prevent another poor cup exit.

Harper made additional signings including Neil Jenkins, a left back from Sutton Utd and Reece Jones on loan from AFC Wimbledon. Ledgister returned as a permanent signing from Sutton but a serious knee injury immediately cut short his season continuing the bad run of serious injuries to key players that undermined the season.

Results did begin to improve through January and February although peppered here and there by inconsistent passages of form. The side managed to get out of the relegation places for the first time rising to the heady heights of 18th place and an improbable escape from the drop looked a possibility. But home form remained dire with only three wins all season. Whatever the reason, it was a trend set in place during the previous season with Hampton having won only 13 of the previous 63 home games.

Coming into the final weeks of the league season, Hampton had a run of three home games followed by the last game away at already relegated Thurrock. The target for safety was 44 points and manager Mark Harper was keen not to leave everything resting on the last game. Two wins out of four would have seen them safe but they contrived to lose all three home fixtures against Salisbury, Welling and Basingstoke which meant they needed a win at Thurrock and for other results to go their way.

Hampton's 2-0 victory at Thurrock was, however, in vain as relegation rivals Havant & Waterlooville and Maidenhead scraped last minute goals to pick up the vital points keeping them out of the relegation places. Hampton were relegated back to the Isthmian Premier on 42 points with Thurrock. Woking and Dartford won promotion.

Forty two ironically was the same number of points that Hampton had won in the previous season when finishing 15th, a record of 10 wins, 12 draws and 20 defeats. Arguably Hampton had not deteriorated over Devonshire's last season and achieved similar results with a less experienced side. Consolation came with a win in the Middlesex Senior Cup Final, 3-2 against Wealdstone at Uxbridge but as consolations went it was pretty meagre compared to losing Conference South status.

When analysing the reasons for relegation it seems clear that the budget constraints were always going to make it a tough season. Long term injuries to key players such as Lovett, Ledgister and Ruby and suspensions added to the need to chop and change line ups.

Some players were not capable of stepping up to Conference South level and a string of early defeats sucked confidence out of the team. The average age of the squad was significantly younger than previous seasons, and in hindsight a little more experience was needed. However, the recruitment of Darren Powell had not stemmed the tide of defeats as had been hoped. Inevitably the manager came in for much criticism. It was his first role as a manager at this level and he tried to stick to ball playing principles when perhaps a more pragmatic strategy was needed. Tactical changes did not always come off. It took a while to find a team that could compete effectively, but a frustrating level of inconsistency remained and when it came to the crunch final games the side failed to deliver. Dave Tarpey ended top scorer with 24 goals, not a bad return for a relegated side but not surprisingly he didn't see his future in the Isthmian League.

Isthmian Premier Division: 2012/13 Season

The obvious concern for manager and supporters alike was that relegation would lead to an exodus of players who wanted to remain at Conference South level. Harper was keen to get some positive backing for the new season.

"I want to hear some positives from the chairman about us trying to get promotion next year and getting some backing to do that. If not, then I might have to re-think my position."

However, it was going to be impossible to retain the whole squad. Dave Tarpey was first out the door joining Farnborough Town and was later followed by Joel Ledgister, heading to Chelmsford City, and Craig Ross who signed for Cambridge Utd as a fulltime professional. Midfielder Josh Huggins was later deemed surplus to requirements and also ended up at Farnborough with Dean Inman who was loaned out to the Hampshire side, unable to command a starting place. Fans were quick to ask why two players who were deemed not good enough for Hampton were good enough for one level above.

Otherwise, Manager Mark Harper was able to retain a good number of the previous season's squad to which was added defenders Max Hustwick (Lewes) and Alan Bray (Sutton Utd), right back Malvin Kamara, former Hampton favourite Gary Holloway (Lewes), and strikers Joey Benjamin (Tonbridge Angels) and Jon Jo Bates (Dagenham & Redbridge). Holloway, who had missed most of the previous season at Lewes through injury, seemed something of a gamble having lost much of his mobility and was never able to show the form of his earlier time at the club.

In contrast to the previous campaign, life back in the Isthmian League could hardly have started more positively with Hampton undefeated in their first ten League and Cup matches, and by the end of September they were leading the table alongside Margate and Bury Town. Charlie Moone was in fine scoring form with nine goals in the first ten games and it took seven games before a single goal was conceded, a club record. The central defensive pairing of Hustwick and Powell supported by Kamara and Jenkins looked to have all the experience lacking in the previous season. Playing that one level lower gave the breathing space that the team needed. Youngsters Tom Hickey and Joe Turner who had come into the team the previous season, were regularly starting alongside Gary Holloway and James Simmonds but for goals the Beavers were very much dependent on Moone. To rectify this Harper brought in ex Leeds Utd striker, Tresor Kandol, the club having pushed the budget to secure him. Kandol had been out of the game for more than a year and never got fit enough to justify the cost and was released a few weeks later.

After two routine wins against lower league opposition, the FA Cup 3rd Qualifying Round trip to Bury Town was going to be much more of a challenge given their league position, but few expected the resulting 4-0 thrashing at the hands of the Suffolk side. It was Hampton's first defeat of the season. On the day, Bury were on their game and deserved their win. Better news came with the return of Joel Ledgister who had not settled at Chelmsford and he immediately scored on his second debut in the 2-1 league win over Lewes. A further 1-0 home win against league leaders Whitehawk in the next match saw Hampton back on top the table and the Bury defeat was quickly forgotten.

Or was it? The next league game away at Wealdstone became, in hindsight, the turning point of the season. Wealdstone were challenging in the top half of the division and were always tough opponents on their own turf. Hampton got off to an excellent start leading 2-0 through Hickey and Ledgister but the game ended with Wealdstone fighting to back to win 3-2 inflicting Hampton first league defeat of the season, not helped by Gary Holloway being sent off.

The Wealdstone result seemed to trigger a crisis of confidence with league form going into a dramatic tailspin. From being second only on goal difference to Whitehawk at the start of November, Hampton lost five and drew two of their next eight games with their only win coming against Wingate & Finchley. To add to the sense of gloom, they were knocked out of the FA Trophy at Chelmsford after a replay going two down in 15 minutes, and then lost to lowly Harrow Borough and bottom placed Carshalton at home on Boxing Day, a game played in terrible conditions which in hindsight was probably better postponed. Other than losing Hickey through suspension for five games after two sendings off, the team stayed very much the same as the one who had got themselves to the top of the league. Confidence just seemed to have drained away.

The bad run of results inevitably placed the spotlight on the management team with old criticisms of the previous season resurfacing. Lack of decent training facilities was highlighted as one possible cause for the slump in form, the main pitch being off limits, overuse and bad weather giving rise to drainage problems. This was probably a factor but not the whole story. Frustration began to build, and the club released a statement over the Christmas period stating that the next three games needed to see a marked improvement, the implication being that if none were seen then the board would be looking for a new manager.

As it turned out the next two games saw two draws against Kingstonian and Lewes before bad weather prevented any further league games until the beginning of February. Whether the board ever intended to take action became somewhat blurred when the Chairman stated to the local press that Harper's job was never in question, the public ultimatum being designed to galvanise some positive reaction from the players.

By early January Hampton had drifted down to 10th place but still mathematically well within sight of a play-off place. Changes were made with Jenkins, Bates and Ledgister all released, and winger Tony Taggart and centre forward Ryan Moss recruited in from Havant & Waterlooville, both experienced players and said to be on top money. However, results did not pick up to any significant extent. In the next 14 games, the side managed only two wins, six defeats and six draws but one of those being a 5-0 win away at Bognor Regis with Moss scoring a hattrick in a makeshift line up due to mounting injury problems. The result and performance were unfortunately a one off. By then Charlie Moone had decided enough was enough and moved to Boreham Wood in the Conference South having scored 24 goals in 40 appearances; no other player managed to get into double figures. The club had something of a sinking feeling about it. By March Harper admitted that the season was over as far as any league honours were concerned.

"At about this time of the season," he said, *"clubs have to decide whether they throw money at the team and go for a final push, or consolidate and look forward to next year, and we come in the latter camp. A lot of managers are in the same position and life has been financially very tough. I have been a*

manager for only a couple of years, but I have been surprised at how much of my time is spent on non-football things. But I am sure I will be here next year, and I am working on keeping the team together until the end of the season and then throughout the summer."

The pitch not at its best

The view was realistic given the league position but perhaps less so about his own role. The Easter Bank holiday fixture at bottom placed Carshalton rounded off a torrid time for Harper, his side losing 3-0 in a game where, to many supporters, it appeared that the team had thrown in the towel from the kick-off, conceding two goals in the first five minutes. It became impossible for the board to ignore what was happening any longer and Harper resigned along with his assistant Andy Smith. Interviewed by the local press Harper stated:

"The internal issues at the club have made it very difficult to do a proper job here and I have my reputation to consider. When football decisions are made without your input, then what can you do?" He added: *"I don't want to go into details but if the club does not sort itself out, I can see it falling further down the leagues, which would be a shame because it is a great club with many great fans and great people who work behind the scenes."*

What were the exact internal issues Harper was referring to were not clear but further cuts in the playing budget were assumed to be the reason. The club had also decided to cut its Capital League side for the next season again presumed to be for financial reasons.

First team coach Paul Barry and veteran defender Darren Powell were put in temporary charge to see out the season with nine games to go, the board deciding to take their time in deciding who would be the next permanent incumbent. Play offs had long gone as an objective although relegation also looked equally unlikely. Barry and Powell saw out the season comfortably enough without creating a significant change in the pattern of results. The season fizzled out to nothingness having had started so promisingly. Hampton finished 13th with 53 points from 42 games. Whitehawk were crowned champions with Concord Rangers, who had finished 5th, promoted through the play offs. For Hampton, the final league placing was solid mid-table but felt like failure given the strong start.

Harper's time in charge at the club will go down as one of the least successful managerial reigns although his record was not too dissimilar to that of Alan Devonshire in the last couple of seasons before his own departure. Relegation in the first year followed by the collapse in results in the second raised the obvious questions about his appointment but taken as a whole the previous three seasons had been beset by financial constraints and the results reflected this. It was a matter of debate whether any other manager could have done a better job with the same limited resources. Hampton were perhaps just reverting to their more natural level. The real mystery was what happened following the Wealdstone defeat as it was largely the same team that had taken Hampton to the top of the league. Moone kept chipping in with goals but other forwards and midfielders found it hard to contribute their share.

Arguably the board left it too late to replace Harper if they had a genuine play off place in mind. The Chairman was personally loyal to Harper, a lifelong friend, and wanted to see if he could pull the results round. Others might not have been so supportive.

The manager vacancy as expected generated a lot of interest. The issue again for the board was whether they could find someone prepared to work on a limited budget who could unearth younger talent that could be moulded into a team that was more than the sum of its parts. When it came to it, some of the potential names were unable to work with the budget and it came down to a choice between the caretakers, Barry and Powell, and another up and coming management pair from two steps below. Again, continuity was felt the best option and Barry and Powell, were confirmed before the end of the season to give them sufficient time to plan for the next campaign. For most supporters this was a popular choice, tinged with the realisation that gone were days of being to compete with the bigger teams in the division. It was the first time that Hampton had appointed joint managers in their history.

I'm very excited to get started," said Paul Barry, *"we're confident of keeping the players we want and adding a few players with the ability and mentality we want at Hampton and Richmond.*

We have a history of encouraging young players through the club and we hope this will continue.

We have shown in the last few weeks that we like to play entertaining football and hopefully we will get the results to go with this."

Manager's Record

Mark HARPER	P	W	D	L	F	A	Pts	Ave	Win%
Combined	98	33	27	38	146	150			33.7
League	75	20	23	32	98	111	83	1.11	26.6
Cup	23	13	4	6	48	39			56.5

Isthmian Premier Division: 2013/14 Season

Although realistic about their chances, Barry and Powell had shown that they could bring through talented young players like Tom Hickey, Joe Turner and 17 year old left back George Wells into the side. Although club captain Matt Ruby and veteran midfielder Gary Holloway departed, much of the squad signed up again for a further season. To these were added strikers, Jordan Rocastle (Wroxham), Charlie Moone, returning from his brief spell at Boreham Wood, Dan Thompson, former Beavers Stuart Lake and Joel Ledgister (back for his third spell), defender Marcus Rose (Maidenhead Utd) and midfielders Tommy Brewer (Lewes), Mo Harkin (Ks) and Rob Carrick (Chertsey

Paul Barry

Town). Dean Inman, although still under contract moved to Hayes & Yeading, then in the Conference South, having once again attracted attention from professional clubs. Darren Powell finally hung up his boots to concentrate on management. Club Chairman Steve McPherson was keen not to overplay his team's chances.

He said,

Joint manager, Darren Powell

"We're all really excited about the season. Paul Barry and Darren Powell have come in and really got their teeth into the job. I think we've put together a tidy squad and, if we make a good start to the season, who knows where it will take us. Perhaps not too many people are mentioning Hampton & Richmond in terms of winning the title due to our poor second half of last season. That's fine by me, it keeps the pressure off. We certainly aren't in the business of throwing money at the team, but there are a lot of positives."

"There are always sides that make the big signings that leave others a little envious, but we're not going to try and match them pound for pound by spending silly money to make sure we compete. We believe this is the right way to do things – the club's security has to come first."

In contrast to the previous season, Hampton took time to find their feet but then built steadily gaining some notable victories along the way to finish pretty much where they had ended up 12 months before. However, this time the momentum was in a forward direction which suggested that the joint managers had grown into the job, learnt through early adversity and shown that they could deliver a solid team which had a much younger average age than previous seasons. It also suggested that they were capable of progressing further, perhaps with an outside chance of a play-off place. Off the field there were also more positive developments as the club secured a long-term lease extension from the Borough and secured new training facilities which had been such a cause for controversy under Mark Harper.

Hampton went into the first home game against Margate with a side weakened by injuries and suspensions having to play a left footed left back, Anson Cousins, at right back, which was not ideal. Frustratingly, Margate scored a last-minute goal to win 2-1. Two draws then followed before an unhappy 3-0 defeat at home to Wealdstone in which Joel Ledgister was sent off for two yellow cards, Tommy Brewer conceded an own goal and keeper Rodney Chiweshe and defender Alan Bray got themselves into a mix up for the third. Hampton were clearly struggling for goals and failed again to score away at Kingstonian when losing 1-0 to former Beaver Ryan Moss' header. Five games and just two goals scored meant that Hampton were plunged straight into the relegation zone and supporters started to wonder just where the first win would come from.

The answer was East Thurrock where the five midfielders from the Kingstonian game were dropped and new signings Ryan Case and Alex Parsons were drafted in from Bournemouth. The performance was not noticeably better but an 81st minute goal by Alan Bray secured a much needed three points. Next up were a much-fancied Maidstone Utd side at home and Hampton were quickly out of the game conceding twice in the first 20 minutes eventually losing 3-1. By now they had scored just four goals in seven league games.

The 1st Qualifying Round of the FA Cup therefore came as something of a respite from the difficult start to the league season with a home draw to near neighbours, Ashford Town (Mx). Despite being 2-0 down, a Joel Ledgister hattrick and a goal from Jordan Rocastle saw Hampton comfortably through to the next round and with some prize money in the bag. A 4-0 win against divisional whipping boys Cray Wanderers followed, although it took until the 74th minute to break the deadlock at which point the floodgates opened. The result said more about Cray than Hampton's improvement as the next game Hampton were on the wrong end of the same score line away at Bognor Regis, sending Hampton back into the bottom four. The joint managers were quick to make changes, bringing in Carshalton defender Justyn Roberts and releasing Ledgister, Case and Matt Reece who had struggled to make an appearance all season.

The Cups seemed to offer better hope with Bedford Town drawn as opponents in the FA Cup. Moone's goal proved to be the winner bringing up next a tie at home against Arlesey Town to whom Hampton had so ignominiously capitulated two seasons' previously, 6-2. This time the tables were turned, and it was Arlesey suffering a heavy defeat, 5-1, with Moone getting a hattrick. Hampton put on their best performance of the season and drew

Charlie Moone

Gloucester City of the Conference North away in the 4th Qualifying Round. The game was played at Cheltenham's Waddon Road ground due to Gloucester City's own pitch being out of action due to flooding. Before that tie could happen, Hampton were back facing Bedford Town this time in the FA Trophy, winning through after a replay, 2-0.

The Gloucester City tie was a real test for Hampton's young side, one that started brightly playing into a strong wind with Moone yet again on the score sheet to give Hampton a 1-0 half time lead. However, Gloucester came out for the second half with more determination and ran out 3-1 winners seeming to have that little bit more stamina than their Isthmian League opponents. Despite the disappointment of missing out on the chance to make the 1st Round proper for only the third time in the club's history, the cup competitions had shown that there was more to be had than just another season of fighting relegation. By the time they faced Gloucester they had had gone on an unbeaten run of 10 games.

Moone in particular was at the heart of the improvement starting to rack up goals on a regular basis including four in the 5-2 defeat of Hendon. In fact, this was to be a run of startling scoring prowess by Moone who had not always been seen as a regular starter in the past. The problem for Barry and Powell was that Moone was the only one scoring with any regularity and there was concern that he could be lost once again to a bigger club. Thankfully, Moone seemed happy at Hampton. A number of strike partners were brought in to spread the goal scoring load: Aaron Wickham and Belal Aite-Oukarim came in but didn't bring the goal threat needed. Luckily Moone kept on going.

Tommy Brewer drives forward

Before the end of the campaign, people were starting to scour the record books as Moone approached first 30 and then 40 goals, not something that had been achieved at the club for more than two decades. In the end Moone didn't quite reach the all-time season record of Syd Carter (1967-8 season, 47) but did chalk up an amazing 40 goals which was an incredible feat considering that Hampton never got out of the bottom half of the League all season.

Despite going out of the FA Trophy 3-1 at Basingstoke, league results distinctly improved with Hampton dragging themselves out of the four relegation spots. Christmas holiday wins over 2nd placed Kingstonian, 4-1, and League leaders Wealdstone, 3-1, showed that on their day Hampton could take on the best in the league. Barry and Powel had to fight off approaches for four of his young players, Moone, Hickey, Turner and Wells but all were prepared to stay.

Recruitment ticked over with the goal shy Dan Thompson heading off to Hayes and Yeading to be replaced by the returning Dave Tarpey, who left the increasingly circus like happenings of Farnborough Town. Ben Harris, a young striker signed from Windsor &

Eton, making an immediate impression. Moone, Tarpey and Harris were all on the score sheet in a comfortable 4-0 win over Carshalton and suddenly Hampton 11th in the League and on a run of nine games unbeaten. And then they went to play title chasing Maidstone Utd on their new 4G pitch.

With injuries and suspensions weighing heavily on the squad, Paul Barry brought in two loan players from Leyton Orient, centre back Alex Finney and midfielder Lawson Okemeji. Despite taking an early lead, the Hampton midfield and defence were run ragged by a much more powerful Maidstone side who looked as if they might score with every attack. And unfortunately, they exploited some rather naïve tactics from the visitors to end up 7-2 winners, the first time Hampton had conceded 7 goals since 1994. It could easily have been double that score if not for some heroics from keeper, Rodney Chiweshe. It was a chastening experience for all involved and form did suffer in the next few games as the side won only one of the next five. The side continued to hover around mid-table, comfortably distanced from the relegation zone but equally comfortably adrift of the play-off spots. A decision was taken to reduce the budget six weeks from the end of the season which seemed a sensible move given that the team was not going to be involved at either business end. Eventually Hampton progressed up to a final position of 12th with 18 wins, 10 draws 18 defeats and 64 points, one place higher and 5 points better than the previous finish.

Popular keeper Rodney Chiweshe

Tom Hickey

The season was topped off with a final flourish winning the Middlesex Senior Cup against league Champions Wealdstone, two from Tarpey and a 30 yard screamer from Tom Hickey early in the second half. Wealdstone were quick to come calling for the services of Hickey and Turner as soon as the season finished.

Looking back, Barry and Powell had a good first season in charge after a rocky start. There was much to like about the style of the side and in the likes of Wells, Turner, Hickey, Wanadio, Harris and Brewer, some very promising prospects who would go on to decent non-league careers in subsequent seasons. Charlie Moone was the obvious standout performance with his 40 goals and cleaned up the end of season awards as was to be expected. Tarpey weighed in with 14 goals.

54 players were used during the season with most appearances from Rodney Chiweshe (56), Joe Turner (55), George Wells (52), Tommy Brewer (49) and Charlie Moone (49). Moone scored 40 out of a total of 109 goals.

On the debit side, Paul Barry admitted that the side could be inconsistent at times being capable of beating some of the stronger sides but failing to impress against lesser opposition - a sign perhaps of inexperience and the limited budget which made it hard to draft in experienced players when beset by injuries and suspensions. For most supporters, there was a feeling that Barry and Powell had stabilised the ship and delivered a season more than up to expectations. Now could they push on and deliver something more?

Isthmian Premier Division: 2014/15 Season

This was to prove another of those tumultuous seasons at the Beveree where everything changed yet again. Stability at non-league level is a luxury few teams enjoy, and Hampton were no different in this respect. However, in hindsight it also heralded a new era of success for the club although few might have thought so given the events that followed.

Barry and Powell knew it was going to be difficult to hold onto some of their up and coming stars and in addition to Hickey and Turner stepping up to the Conference South, Dave Tarpey and James Simmonds followed suit by moving up a league to join Maidenhead Utd and Hemel Hempstead respectively. Although he played most of the pre-season, club captain Stuart Lake opted to take on a player-coach role at Wingate and Finchley which meant the loss of the teams most experienced player. Incoming were defender Max Hustwick, back for a second spell, midfielders Jesse Kewley-Graham from Wycombe Wanderers, Billy Adcock from local football, wide midfielder Michael Bryan from Hendon and speedy winger Jerome Federico from Northwood. Up front former Staines forward Paul Butler was signed to vie for the goalscoring honours with Moone and Harris. During pre-season came the devastating news that 'keeper Rodney Chiweshe had ruptured his Achilles tendon playing 5-a-side football, ruling him out of active sport for the next 12 months. Finding an adequate replacement at this late stage proved to be a difficult task although the season eventually started with Wayne Carter signed from Wealdstone in possession of the gloves. The lack of continuity in this vital position was one of the reasons the side began to struggle.

In the first league game Hampton were drawn away at Margate, one of the fancied teams for the season where manager Terry Brown had reputedly been given a big budget to secure promotion. It was a tough test both on paper and on the pitch with a strong breeze gusting straight down the Crabble's exposed ground. Hampton gave a good account of themselves but succumbed to a 77th minute goal and, although always under pressure, showed enough spirit and effort to suggest that they were going to be competitive. Wingate & Finchley were first up at home the following Tuesday, a side that had been reprieved from relegation the previous season. A Charlie Moone penalty saw the sides equal 1-1 going into the half time break. There had been no hints of the collapse that was to follow but in a disastrous second half display three goals were conceded without reply, Hampton falling to a poor 4-1 defeat and the loss of defender Justyn Roberts to injury. Powell spoke to the press after and was clearly upset by the performance:

"Let's be clear, Tuesday night was so poor......you can't put in such a bad performance in your first home game of the season, it sets the wrong tone."

Unfortunately, he was right. More misery was to come losing at home to newly promoted Witham 4-2 to one of the sides expected to struggle at the wrong end of the table. Further defeats followed away at Maidstone, 2-0, and home to Grays Athletic, 4-0, meaning that Hampton had lost their first four league games for the first time in 33 years. Undoubtedly the loss of some key players left the side short of experience and bite in midfield. Kewley-Graham who had been placed on a long term contract such were his apparent credentials looked out of his depth once the season proper was under way and was quickly dropped. Carter was swiftly replaced by Jack Norton in goal and the pack was shuffled from game to game to find a combination that would stem the flow of goals.

The game against Lewes, who similarly had no wins, already looked like a crunch six pointer but to supporters' relief goals from Moone and Wells saw Hampton home 2-1 despite going down to 10 men. Three more points were picked up away at Harrow Borough with the same score line, this time Harris and Dunn contributing the goals and the mini-revival continued with a creditable 2-2 draw at Dulwich Hamlet with Academy product Paris Mason scoring the equaliser deep into added time. But just seven points from the first eight games left Hampton languishing in 21st place and the worst goals against record in the division. To make matters worse, Paul Butler broke his ankle away from football and failed to reappear after the second game against Wingate & Finchley.

Next up were Leiston who had started the season strongly and with the score 2-2 at half time everything was to play for. Six goals rattled in in the second period with Leiston winning out 6-4 leaving supporters shell-shocked and fearing the worst for the following Saturday's FA Cup visit to lowly VCD Athletic. The pressure was well and truly on the joint managers after the Leiston debacle made worse by the loss of Ben Harris to injury. VCD were as ordinary a team as Hampton could have hoped to meet in the Cup but they handed them a 2-0 lead in a toothless performance before clawing back to 2-2 through goals from Wells and Mason. Having done the hard work Hampton then threw it all away conceding a third headed goal to VCD who barely got out of their half all game. It proved the final straw for Barry and Powell who resigned immediately after the final whistle. It was only early September.

Their record of P71, W31, D16, L24 was by no means the worst in recent history but just two wins in nine games in the new season and the leakiest of defences was flirting with dismissal and the axe duly fell with the FA Cup exit. Chairman Steve McPherson spoke to the local press:

"It was not nice a nice conversation to have as we as a board have only good things to say about them both. I feel that the fact that they have come to this decision speak volumes for them both. They could have continued but for the good of the club they want to allow another manager the opportunity to come in try to turn things around.

For that, they need enormous credit. They will both be welcome at Hampton & Richmond any time. I feel tonight the players need to be asking themselves some tough questions. Their performances have not help and I feel they have left themselves and Paul and Darren down at times."

Dowson and Chairman, Steve McPherson

McPherson moved swiftly to fill the gap with 44 year old former Walton & Hersham and Kingstonian manager, Alan Dowson. Dowson had left Kingstonian at the end of the previous season having narrowly missed out on promotion and after five years in the job. An ex-professional left back at Millwall and Fulham, Dowson was known for this passionate and sometime eccentric devotion to the game and his ability to squeeze out as much as possible, and sometimes more, from a limited budget. As his No2 he brought with him his long-term associate, football commentator, Martin Tyler, himself a former amateur centre forward with Corinthian Casuals whom Dowson had met when coaching junior football. As unlikely a combination as it was, Geordie Dowson was very much the "boss" and Tyler the assistant. Added to the coaching staff was Reserve Team assistant manager, Ian Dyer.

For those who know how the story ends, Dowson's success at the club was perhaps only a matter of time. However, the immediate weeks and months following his appointment became one of the most frenetic in the club's history with a bewildering turnover of players brought in and turned around as Dowson tried to find a winning formula. By the end of the season 71 players had appeared for Hampton during the season, 20 of which played one game or

less. To fair to Dowson, he came into find a team low on confidence and in many positions low on ability sitting second bottom of the division, looking down rather than up. It was really a question of saving the club from relegation and then looking to progress from there if possible. There was no questioning the level of enthusiasm and energy Dowson brought to the job nor the depths of his contacts and ability to persuade players to join the club and share his vision. But to some it all looked a bit hit and miss.

His first game less than 24 hours after being appointed was a visit to Hendon where out of favour midfielder Kewley-Graham[14] started for the first time in a number of matches and remarkably scored after just 37 seconds, Hampton coming away in the end with a 2-2 draw. Nonetheless, Hampton were staring up at the league in 22nd place; it looked a steep climb back to safety.

Alan Dowson

Dowson had drafted in experienced centre half Kieran Murphy, a player Dowson had with him at Kingstonian, from Hemel Hempstead on dual registration, to play at Hendon. Murphy was the first of a rich pipeline of players who made the trip from Hemel to Hampton with fellow centre back

---

[14] Kewley-Graham didn't feature long term in Dowson's plans but refused to go out on loan. His contract was paid up in January 2015.

Moussa Diarra next to appear for the home game against East Thurrock along with further new signings Tom Collins, a forward from Wealdstone, midfielder Saheed Sankoh and defender Thomas Opoku. The Hemel players were clearly of a better quality but were subject to recall which made establishing a settled side difficult. Nonetheless, the hoped-for new manager bounce was evident as Hampton went on to win the next three games elevating them to a relatively comfortable 12th place and importantly conceding only one goal on the way.

However, the home game against Leatherhead brought the run of good form to an unexpected and abrupt end, with Hampton on the end of a 5-1 hammering, followed by a poor performance away at Tonbridge Angels where Hampton went down 2-0. Fingers were being pointed at keeper Jack Norton who had made errors in both games and Dowson decided enough was enough and brought in Ronnie Worster for two games before negotiating the loan of 18-year-old Brentford keeper Mark Smith who started to add some solidity to the back line. But there were still difficult times to be experienced including a 6-0 defeat at Wealdstone in the Middlesex Senior Cup where Hampton conceded five goals before half time, and a 3-0 defeat in the league away at Met Police. Following the dire performance at Police, Dowson gave it both barrels in his comments to the press:

"We are all over the shop." He said. *"There is a defeatist attitude in the dressing room and the whole club stinks of it. When you are nine games in as a new manager you are looking for people to impress you. I'm not saying everyone else has been terrible, but Saheed Sankoh and Moussa Diarra have been the only two in a team of 11 to have impressed me. That is not very many people. This has been going on for years. There has been relegation from the Conference South, we've finished in the bottom half of the Ryman Premier and we're a bottom of the table now. I'll not lose anything by throwing the kids in because I've then got eight or nine days – which I haven't had before – to sort out a team.*

There will be a lot of comings and goings. I wish the players who leave all the best, but I'll be ringing the changes. I'm at the end of my tether now. If I have to play the kids at the weekend I will. We have done unbelievably well to get five wins and a draw since I've been in charge, but I took on a relegation scrap and we are still in one. People say I do all this stuff for charity, but they will see a different side to me now."

Behind the scenes, Dowson felt that there were disruptive cliques in the dressing room which needed to be weeded out. Former captain Billy Jeffreys was released as was Tommy Brewer, Harry Mills, Luke Wanadio and Gareth Chendlik. Incoming were a mixture of loans and permanent signings including Archie Nkumu from Concord Rangers, Nick Bignall from Sutton Utd, Ola Williams from Harrow Borough, Tashen Adeyinka and Louis Morrison from Maidenhead, and Jake Rose from Farnborough. With so many changes it took a time for the new players to gel and a 3-0 home defeat by Grays Athletic saw Hampton out of the FA Trophy at the first time of asking. League form continued to be patchy although Hampton surprised many with a 2-0 home win over league leaders Margate which kept them reasonably clear of the drop zone in 12th place. Dowson had rung the changes but still felt he was in need of three or four more permanent signings. Ex K's centre back Matty Drage came in to be paired with Kieran Murphy to try and cut out the many goals conceded from crosses during the season.

But the Margate victory at the end of November was to be the last win before managing a 2-1 win at home to Harrow Borough on 17th January, Drage with a long range winner, and Hampton had slipped back down the table.

More players came and went and by early December 57 players had appeared in the red and blue. Some left and came back and left again. Some were familiar faces like James Simmomds who returned on loan from Hemel, others barely registered before disappearing into the footballing ether. As the season wore on, Dowson managed to attract some of the players that would go on to form the backbone of next season's side: Tom Jelley from Tooting & Mitcham, Kieran Murphy who signed permanently from Hemel, goalkeeper Seb Brown and attacking midfielder Brendan Kiernan from Ebbsfleet, initially on loan. Duncan Culley also returned for a second loan spell.

The Harrow victory was followed up with a narrow 1-0 win over Dulwich Hamlet but it was to take another nine games before a further win came along at home in a relegation six pointer against Hornchurch. The win left Hampton six points clear of the relegation places in 19th needing 12 points from the last games to reach safety. A loss at Enfield saw Hampton drop to one place above the four relegation spots before four wins in the final run in of games took them back up to a final finish of 15th place.

The final record of Played 46, Won 16, Drawn 9, Lost 21 and 57 points was 11 points worse and three places lower than achieved in the previous season. Hampton had the fourth worst defensive record in the division conceding 79 times.

Maidstone were crowned champions with Margate promoted through the play offs.

Dowson had nonetheless achieved the objective of maintaining Hampton's Isthmian Premier status and was awarded with an extended two year contract. However, the road to safety was a bumpy one, having to rebuild a team from scratch after the dreadful start under Barry and Powell, begging and borrowing players from other clubs and regularly shuffling the pack all within a still limited budget. It wasn't for the want of trying but the whole season was never an easy watch for supporters who had never seen so many players pass through the Beveree gates. Thankfully better days were just around the corner.

Managers' Record

Paul BARRY & Darren POWELL	P	W	D	L	F	A	Pts	Ave	Win %
Combined	79	33	15	31	137	135			41.8
League	64	23	14	27	98	109	83	1.3	35.9
Cup	15	10	1	4	39	26			66.6

Dowson Unbound: 2015-2018

Isthmian League Premier: 2015/16 Season

Pre-season saw Moone, Murphy, Sinclair, Federico, Kamara, Richmond and Jelley all retained, with Dowson adding further experience to the squad with the likes of ex Brentford midfielder Eddie Hutchinson from Maidenhead, and Seb Brown who signed on a permanent basis. Perhaps the most important signing was Josh Casey from Dowson's old club Kingstonian. Casey was originally recruited as a midfielder but later settled into the left back position from which he captained the side. He brought a strong winning mentality that chimed with Dowson's own approach and in the next two seasons was rarely if ever out of the starting line-up unless injured or suspended. Somewhat cheekily, he was known in the dressing room as "son of Dowson."

The Hemel Hempstead pipeline continued to be a fertile source of recruitment with out of favour striker Nicke Kabamba taken on a three month loan, and also midfielder Ryan Newman. Joe Hicks a young centre back from Corinthian Casuals was also brought in to bolster options. Competing up front was well travelled striker Richard Pacquette who had played briefly on loan for the club ten years before under Alan Devonshire. Of the side that started the first league fixture away at Harrow Borough four were ex Hemel players, Murphy, Diarra, Newman and Kabamba but it was club stalwart Charlie Moone that got the Beavers' only goal in a closely fought 1-1 draw at Earlsmead.

Early results proved mixed with just one win over East Thurrock at home in the first five games. Defensively the side was sound but goals were hard to come by with Moone and Kabamba managing just three goals between them. Draws against some of the weaker teams in the division, VCD Athletic and Lewes, both destined to be relegated, had

Josh Casey

Dowson immediately reaching for his contact book in order to fill the gaps opening up due to injuries, suspensions and indifferent form. Two wins against local rivals Met Police and Staines however saw Hampton up to 8th place, so within sight of the five key promotion play off places, albeit that Dowson had been hoping for a better start to the season. A lacklustre 1-1 draw with Burgess Hill Town, another side that struggled all season, was followed by the midweek visit of Lewes to the Beveree, with winless Lewes languishing in 23rd place. Joe Hicks, in for the injured Murphy, was sent off in the first half conceding a freekick that led to Lewes' first goal and the 10 men were mercilessly turned over by a further three goals from the visitors in the second period. The following Saturday, Hicks was again at fault conceding a late penalty to see Dulwich Hamlet through in the 1st Qualifying Round of the FA Cup. Supporters' knives were beginning to be sharpened once again.

When Hampton travelled to Champion Hill to face Dulwich in the league just 10 days later, Dowson gave a debut to young midfielder Harry Taylor brought in on loan from Barnet. Moone, Pacquette and Sinclair scored Hampton's goals in an entertaining 3-3 draw, the first time all season that the side had scored more than twice in a game. Dowson was still not happy with his side and after a 3-1 defeat away to league leaders Leiston he described the performance as "crap" accusing certain players of coasting. Further changes were deemed necessary, and Dowson brought winger Shaquille Hippolyte-Patrick and long-term target Brendan Kiernan in on loan from National League sides Sutton Utd and Bromley respectively. Kiernan had briefly appeared on loan the previous season whilst at Ebbsfleet and Dowson continued to tempt the skilful

Nicke Kabamba

forward with the promise of more regular football compared to Bromley where he had been in and out of the side. Despite the inconsistent results and performances, the league table remained a closely run thing with Hampton in 8th place, but with just one point covering 3rd to 11th place any number of sides were still in contention.

The injection of new blood appeared to have the right effect when both new recruits appeared in a 5-0 home win over Hendon, although Hendon had been reduced to nine men by the end of the game. This uptick in performance proved to be no fluke as the Beavers followed up with an emphatic 6-1 away win at Merstham. Noticeably, these two victories saw Moussa Diarra score four goals, two in each game, his aerial dominance was to become a crucial factor as the season wore on.

The draw for the FA Trophy First Qualifying round saw Hampton once again pitched against Lewes, this time under new management. After a largely eventless 0-0 draw at the Dripping Pan, Hampton won the replay 2-1 with two late goals from Charlie Moone in for the injured Kabamba. Dowson also made a change in goal with Brentford loanee Mark Smith coming in for Seb Brown whose form had been patchy and cause for concern amongst some supporters. Next through the door was another of Hemel Hempstead's unloved squad, attacking wide midfielder, Jamal Lowe, who debuted in a 4-0 Middlesex Senior Cup win over Bedfont & Feltham. It was clear from the start that 21 year old Lowe had something special about him yet he was struggling to get any game time at Hemel. Like many young players he had started with a league club, in his case Barnet, had early success and then fell out of favour when a new manager arrived. A number of loans followed before Barnet released him and he drifted into part time football at St Albans City and Hemel. Rather than a loan, this was a permanent signing and as it turned out, it was one of the most important signings the club was to make in its history; but that was to come.

Lowe immediately contributed to the goals for total in the next round of the FA Trophy in a 3-1 win over AFC Sudbury giving Hampton a plum home draw in the next round against

National League side Maidstone Utd. Despite a strong performance Hampton eventually succumbed to a 90th minute goal from Jay May but the recent forward momentum was not dissipated as Dowson' side went on to win seven games on the bounce, six in the league, propelling the Beavers up to 2nd place behind Dulwich Hamlet. It was clear that Lowe and Kabamba brought out the best in each other scoring 9 goals between them in those seven games, Kabamba five and Lowe four. In his previous 14 games Kabamba had netted four times in total. Their scoring exploits did not let up for the rest of the season and Dowson made Kabamba's signing permanent early in the New Year. Quite how Hemel managed to let these players through their grasp remains one of the mysteries of recent non-league football. Brendan Kiernan's deal was also made permanent whilst Smith and Taylor's loan deals came to an end. Dowson dipped back into the loan market bringing in Reading keeper George Legg to replace Smith although was still hopeful that he could persuade Brentford to allow Smith back for a further period. Legg was not the same commanding presence as Smith and his loan was not extended after a near disastrous performance in the wind effected 4-3 victory over Leiston, Legg conceding three almost identical goals from corners.

Jamal Lowe

By the New Year, the promotion battle was beginning to boil down to a handful of sides. Hampton went top of the table in mid-January for the first time following a 4-0 away win at Canvey Island, with Dulwich Hamlet, East Thurrock and Tonbridge Angels following close behind. The one side that hadn't really featured on anyone's radar was Bognor Regis who had had not appeared in the play-off positions all season but were now mounting a charge. Hampton faced two crucial games at home to Tonbridge Angels followed by a trip to the south coast and Bognor the following Saturday. Despite taking a two goal lead over Tonbridge, the nerves began to jangle when the visitors earned a 90th minute equaliser through Nathan Elder. Worse was to come at Bognor despite the home side having a man sent off after 50 minutes. Rather than Hampton taking advantage, the home side spurred on by the supposed injustice of the red card scrambled a winner dropping Hampton down to 3rd place with Dulwich now back on top.

Dowson still was not content with the squad and continued to look for additions to push the promotion challenge that bit harder. Mark Smith came back in goal on loan till the end of the season and midfield was boosted by the arrival of Leon Solomon from Wingate and Tom Beere from AFC Wimbledon partly to cover a long term injury to Dean Sinclair. Form returned with a run of five consecutive wins which saw Hampton back in top spot and four points clear before a disastrous 4-1 away defeat at Kingstonian on Good Friday. Bognor were nine points behind but with five games in hand having lost games to postponements and FA Trophy commitments. The league title was within reach for Hampton if they could win all of their last four games but it would also need Bognor to drop points as they were the only side that could overtake them mathematically. Sadly, for Bognor, this meant cramming in several league games into a very short period playing three times a week which took its inevitable toll. In the space of five days over the end of March and beginning of April they lost three games in a row which meant that Hampton would be champions if they could take 10 points from their last four games. Bognor still had six to play but on paper all very winnable matches. Similarly, Hampton had three relatively easy games against Brentwood Town, Farnborough and Grays Athletic all sides in the bottom reaches of the table. Dowson's side did a professional job and won all three comfortably.

The only tricky fixture was the last of the season at home to Enfield Town when 2,300 fans crowded into an extremely tense but hopeful Beveree stadium. Enfield were themselves pushing for a play-off place and needing a win on the last day of the season to reach 5th place providing Dulwich Hamlet lost. To make matters even more tense Hampton could afford to lose the game providing Bognor did not make up Hampton's four goal difference advantage against Hendon.

Alan Dowson was reported as saying:

"I've told the wife if we don't [win] I'll be back at 5pm. If we do? I'll be seeing her on Wednesday."

A tense first half ended goalless with Hampton perhaps having the better of the precious few chances on offer. At halftime Enfield were spurred on by the news that Dulwich were losing at Needham Market which meant a win for them would see them

Martyn Tyler and Dowse with the Championship Trophy

move into 5th place. Bognor were however only drawing 0-0 against Hendon so providing some level of cushion for the Beavers. But as the second period wore on worrying news started to emerge from Nyewood Lane as Bognor started to chip away the goals advantage, 1-0, 2-0, 3-0 then incredibly 4-0 up and back equal on goal difference. Everyone in the Beveree now knew that nothing less than a draw was the absolute must, everyone except Enfield who piled on the pressure bringing several great saves out of Mark Smith who was most observers Man of the Match. Hampton rarely did easy but, in the end, Enfield could not find their way through and Hampton clung on for the vital point which saw the league Trophy handed over amongst jubilant celebrations on the pitch.

For the record the team: 1 Mark Smith, 2 Tom Jelley, 3 Josh Casey, 4 Kieran Murphy, 5 Moussa Diarra, 6 Leon Solomon, 7 Shaquille Hippolyte-Patrick (Joe Hicks 82'), 8 Tom Beere, 9 Nicke Kabamba, 10 Brendan Kiernan, 11 Jamal Lowe Subs: 12 Eddie Hutchinson, 13 Martin Brennan, 14 Joe Hicks, 15 Charlie Moone, 16 Jerome Federico

Hampton finished the season with a record of: P46 W28 D10 L7 F105 A52 Pts 95 one point ahead of Bognor. However, it was Dulwich Hamlet that were promoted through the play offs beating Bognor in the final.

Despite over 100 goals being scored no one player reached 20 in the season. Kabamba led the table on 19, followed closely by Lowe and Moone on 15, Diarra on 14 and Kiernan on 12. This showed that the team was not dependent on just one source for its success but the impact of Diarra, Lowe and Kabamba was clearly key in changing Hampton's fortunes. Reflecting on the achievement Alan Dawson said,

"We were rock bottom 18 months ago when Martin and I walked in – we knew it was a massive job with a dressing room that was factional and dominated by strong individuals. We still gave everybody a chance despite having an idea very quickly of who needed to move on, those chances were short-lived because time was not on our side."

Some clubs suggested that Hampton had "splashed the cash" with some of their signings but the reality was that the budget was far from being the largest in the division but somewhere in the top half and a play-off place was always a realistic target. The fact was that Dowson was a past master at working his contacts to find the deals other managers perhaps missed out on, often at little cost to the club, particularly in the loan market. Dowson was tireless in scouting out players and whilst inevitably some of them proved not to be up to scratch, his eye for a decent player was usually pretty spot on. His reward for delivering the title was a renewed two year contract. Dowson was named Isthmian League Manager of the Season. It was hard not to agree that this was thoroughly deserved.

National League South: 2016/17 Season

The return to the National League South, as it was now known, after a four year absence was something for the club to contemplate with great pride and no little optimism. Could Dowson go one better than club legend Alan Devonshire and perhaps take Hampton up to the next level? Realistically it was understood that a further promotion was not likely to be on the cards first time of asking and that there was a limit to how far the club could stretch the budget in a division where Hampton simply could not compete with some of the "bigger" clubs. Nonetheless the board did agree an increase in the playing budget and had expectations that Hampton would be more than also-rans in the division.

In those four years the National League South had seen quite a turnover of sides with just seven clubs remaining from when Hampton last graced its ranks. Ebbsfleet, Dartford and Chelmsford looked to be the early bookies' favourites with a strong challenge expected from Maidenhead Utd now back under the control of Alan Devonshire. Poole and Hungerford Town were complete unknowns promoted from the Southern League but expected to struggle having never reached this level before in their respective histories.

As ever squad changes had to be managed with Moussa Diarra attracting a move to National League Barrow for full time football. No one was that surprised that a bigger club came calling given his dominant performances during the previous season. Nor was it a great surprise when Charlie Moone announced his departure to Slough Town given the more peripheral role he had played following the rise of Lowe and Kabamba. He left as the club's second highest goal scorer of all time with 118 goals in 257 games, just over one goal every other game which was impressive at any level of the game. Smith and Beere returned to their parent clubs as expected.

Inbound recruitment saw the arrival of all action midfielder Harold Odametey from Kingstonian, goalkeeper Aaron Howe and central defender Jay Gasson both from Basingstoke, striker Christian Jolley from Margate (a player that Dowson had discovered whilst at Ks), veteran striker Giuseppe Sole from Woking and former Beaver, Nathan Collier, from Eastbourne Borough. Most of the previous season's squad also returned so on paper it looked a much stronger team overall which was reflected in pre-season friendly victories over Sutton Utd, Aldershot Town and Salford City.

The opening league fixture saw Hampton travel to Bishop's Stortford in blazing early August sunshine. Stortford had finished the previous season in mid table so would be a good test of how Hampton might match up in the division. It turned out to be a tight game with few chances for either side but a penalty from Tom Jelley secured the three points for the Beavers. Jelley was on penalty duty again in the next game converting in a 3-1 home win over Eastbourne Borough with Jamal Lowe scoring twice. The only fly in the ointment was an injury to Aaron Howe which saw him replaced by Billy Bishop who then deputised for the next three league games. Seb Brown was drafted back as cover.

Given the good start it was something of a disappointment to lose the next game 2-1 against fellow promoted side East Thurrock but this setback was quickly forgotten with a run of five wins and two draws in the next seven games pushing Hampton well into contention the early league table behind Maidenhead Utd. The run was brought to an end by another unexpected home defeat this time by Whitehawk with Nathan Collier earning a late red card.

The FA Cup early qualifying rounds saw Hampton with a comfortable away draw at Dunstable Town where they ran out 7-1 winners having been 5-0 up at half time. This earned another away draw at Taunton Town, a side two divisions below in the Southern League Division 1 South & West, a game where Hampton were strong favourites although Taunton were something of an unknown quantity. On their best form Hampton should have seen this game out with ease but despite dominating possession Taunton's physicality and a pitch with the grass left deliberately long to frustrate Hampton's passing game saw the nerves creep into the Beaver's performance. A second half penalty gave Taunton an unexpected 2-1 victory although they were undoubtedly a better side than their league position suggested. Dowson whose Cup record was less than stellar, was typically apoplectic about the defeat.

"Yesterday was THE worst day of my two years at the club, I'm devastated over the result and I shan't rest until I've sorted it out. I can only apologise to the fans and the board, they travelled all that way to see that, and it was nowhere near good enough. I was in my office from nine this morning to start sorting the back four out as I barely slept. We can't go on conceding like this as it's costing us, if we want to be successful, we have to tighten things up. I'll be making some phone calls to see who I can get in to improve things in defence."

True to his word, Dowson brought in defender Louis John on loan from Sutton Utd for the next league game at home to Poole Town who themselves were having an impressive start to the season. Kieran Murphy was dropped to the bench but the 2-0 defeat didn't show the improvement that Dowson had sought, Michael Kamara conceding another penalty. But Hampton remained in 3rd place with the prospect of pitching themselves against league leaders Maidenhead Utd who had won 12 of their 15 league games and were building a commanding points advantage. A crowd of 1146, the largest of the season, saw an exciting and hard-fought game won 3-2 by the Magpies who showed their power and class despite Hampton pushing them hard throughout. Once again Dowson lamented, "we can't defend," as his side slipped to their fourth home league defeat in a row. Not so the case away from home where Hampton went undefeated in the league until early December.

At the top end of the pitch the dynamic duo of Lowe and Kabamba were still riding high sharing over 30 goals between them so it was more than expected that scouts were flocking to the Beveree casting their eyes over the strike partners. Lowe was called up to the England C team and Kabamba put into the reserve squad for the same, the first time any Hampton player had been recognised at this level. Within the club it was no secret that Lowe was attracting attention from both EFL and National League clubs and that Jamal was keen to move back to full-time professional football.

Dowson and the club recognised this and agreed that they would help him take the step up in return for which Lowe had agreed to extend his contract with the Beavers in the close season. Firm bids came in from Eastleigh of the National League and Portsmouth who were then in the EFL Division 2 with Lowe finally deciding that he would sign for Portsmouth on a pre contract basis. Although the initial fee was relatively modest, Chairman Steve McPherson negotiated a sell on clause which was to have a deal more relevance in seasons to come as Lowe took his opportunity at Portsmouth with both hands and moved his way up the divisions to Wigan Athletic and Swansea City in the Championship. Kabamba was not far behind as within weeks Portsmouth decided to take a gamble on reuniting the two friends at Fratton Park. Again, a small fee was paid coming at a time when the club's financial position was beginning to show some strain.

On the pitch Murphy and Gasson were dropped to the bench and replaced by Kamara and the versatile Collier to stem some of the goals conceded, although in truth results proved a little mixed and Murphy and Gasson were reunited in defence as the league moved into the Christmas holiday period with Hampton still placed handily in 4th place after a 4-0 win at home to St Albans City. The one position that remained a headache was in goal. Aaron Howe gave mixed performances and was prone to the odd error which undermined his defence and inevitably the confidence of his manager. Whilst Billy Bishop was given the gloves for the minor cup games, Dowson did not see him as a long term solution and decided to dip once again into the loan market bringing in Charlie Grainger from Orient on a month's loan. When that expired Bishop was drafted back in for another four games before Dowson secured a longer-term loan for West Ham's Sam Howes. Howes immediately showed his worth to the team saving a penalty on his debut away at Bath City in a 1-1 draw and became a vital component to Dowson's side for the rest of the season. Loan deals were also struck with Barnet, then in the EFL Division 2, for young midfielders Harry Taylor and Wesley Fonguck and then for striker Alfie Pavey from Millwall. Duncan Culley also re-joined the club to add some additional fire power now that Kabamba had moved on.

The obvious question was how much Hampton would suffer from the loss of Lowe and Kabamba's goal threat. The answer was a slow drift off in league wins such that Hampton moved out of the play off positions but remained in contention in a chasing group outside the top five. Three weeks without a game in January due to postponements did nothing for momentum or cashflow. Pavey did not seem to have the striking prowess of a Kabamba and on expiry of his loan Dowson rang the changes with the more experienced Shamir Mullings brought in on loan from Forest Green Rovers. But Mullings, like Pavey, only managed one goal in a handful of games. By the end of the season the club's top scorers remained Nicke Kabamba on 22 with Jamal Lowe on 20 despite having played 10 games less than the third placed marksman Brendan Kiernan on 20.

Off the pitch, the news in February that Club President Alan Simpson had passed away aged 87 brought a sombre mood to the club. Whilst Alan had not been in the best of health it still came as a great shock to the Hampton community. Few could doubt that Hampton owed its very existence as a senior club to Alan and were fortunate that he decided to walk down Station Road to watch a game all those years ago in 1966. A fitting farewell to Alan was held on a cold and damp February day at the Beveree with moving ceremony with speeches from family and friends including his godson, Jacques Le Bars and comedian Paul Merton.

Whilst automatic promotion was not considered a realistic possibility, Hampton's form kept them in contention but stubbornly just outside the four play-off positions. However, it started to become clear toward the final weeks of the season that two of the play-off contenders, newly promoted Poole Town and Hungerford Town who sat in 5th and 6th places, did not have the necessary ground grading to participate in the play offs, the League eventually deciding that they would extend the play off places down to 7th in the hope of finding a suitably qualified team. Whilst harsh on Poole and Hungerford, and causing much controversy across the league, the ruling opened the door for Hampton and Wealdstone who were chasing the final play-off spot. Hampton already knew that their 'B' grading was sufficient having carried out extensive work before the Hayes & Yeading final in 2008. Ironically Wealdstone also fell foul of the grading requirement despite frantic attempts to meet the upgrade deadline. The way seemed open for the Beavers but this still required Hampton to secure 7th place. The League decided extending the play offs below 7th place was pushing it a little too far so 8th was not going to do the job.

The tension of a promotion push was therefore back on with the season going down to the wire with Hampton needing to win their last home game against a lowly Concord Rangers side who had nothing to play for. Nonetheless, it was a nervy game won narrowly through a rare Nathan Collier header in the first half. It was enough to secure 7th place and a place in the play offs where Hampton were drawn to face Ebbsfleet Utd in a two leg tie, Ebbsfleet having finished in runners-up spot. Dartford and Chelmsford City faced each other in the other tie.

The final table read:

PL 42 W 19 D 12 L11 F81 A56 Pts 69

two points outside the top five which would have ordinarily been the cut off point for play off qualification.

Both league fixtures against Ebbsfleet had finished in 1-1 draws but in the final league table Ebbsfleet finished with 27 more points than Hampton so there were no illusions that Hampton were clear underdogs. Moreover, injuries were taking their toll of the squad with Tom Jelley, Josh Casey, Brendan Kiernan and Harold Odametey carrying knocks, but all were pressed into action in front of 1,689 hopeful supporters in the first leg at the Beveree.

Ebbsfleet took an early lead with an unfortunate double deflection past the wrong-footed Howes. A clearly unfit Odametey limped out of the game after just 17 minutes with a recurrence of a hamstring injury, a gamble that did not pay off, to be replaced by Sam Gallagher. Worse was to follow when Ebbsfleet converted a soft penalty just before half time. However, Duncan Culley pulled one back within two minutes as the Ebbsfleet keeper spilled a Christian Jolley shot. With no further goals Ebbsfleet took a slender 2-1 lead into the next leg where injury problems continued to beset Hampton as Duncan Culley broke down in the warm-up and was replaced up front by Nathan Collier placing faith in his versatility perhaps a little too far. Again, Ebbsfleet took a 1-0 lead forcing Dowson to take the bold step of throwing on Jerome Federico and Shaquille Hippolyte Patrick in the second half in search of the goals needed to claw back the tie. The plan nearly worked with Federico who had made only two starts all season reviving some of the form that had made him a fans' favourite the season before. Federico's deflected shot made it 1-1 but a late winner for Ebbsfleet settled the tie 4-2 on aggregate and the season was done and dusted. Some compensation was gained when Ebbsfleet were promoted through the play off final, no disgrace losing to the eventual winners who were perhaps more ready to take the step up to the National League.

What fans did not realise was that behind the scenes the club's position was becoming as financially precarious off the field as it was on it with the threadbare squad. From the beginning of the year, it was clear that the budget could not be sustained and only the transfers of Lowe and Kabamba gave some much needed breathing space. In the background, the Supporters' Trust had been working with the former Chairman Graham Wood to see if further funding could be introduced via the Trust alongside existing shareholders. Wood had now ended his stint at Gateshead having just missed out on promotion to the Football League. The Trust with Wood's backing agreed to match the directors pound for pound on new investment but despite an initial cash injection from the Trust as a good faith gesture, existing directors were unable to respond.

But other plans were afoot. The death of Alan Simpson in February also started a dialogue between Wood, the Trust and Alan Simpson's godson Jacques Le Bars about a longer-term solution should existing directors not have the desire to continue funding another season. Towards the end of April, the Supporters' Trust had helped fund wages to keep the ship afloat and there was real concern that the financial uncertainty could

New former Chairman, Graham Wood

see the departure of Alan Dowson and most of his squad once the season was finished. It was agreed that the new investment consortium would wait until the play offs were out of the way before making their bid public. Dowson was fully aware what was waiting in the wings but wanted to see a resolution as soon as possible. Had Hampton won promotion that would have created a whole new set of issues but the Ebbsfleet defeats quickly took that dilemma off the table.

The proposal was tabled just days after the second leg tie and was voted through by the board in the middle of May. In return for substantial investment, it was proposed that Graham Wood would return as Chairman with Jacques Le Bars as Vice Chairman. Another former Chairman, Richard Parsons, agreed to become General Manager with the Trust remaining as a board member also. Whilst all existing directors were invited to remain on board only Kevin Childs and Chas Milner did so with Steve McPherson and David Sines, Vice Chairman deciding to step down.

"We would like to thank Steve for his leadership and hard work to get Hampton back into the upper reaches of National League South", said Wood in his press release.

"It's great for him to go out on a high at the end of a very successful first season back and we can only hope we maintain the same momentum."

"Hampton is a close-knit family and, in this regard, it is wonderful that Jacques has agreed to join the board. I'm sure Alan Simpson would have been happy to see his involvement."

"It was a logical step to hand on the baton at this time. The club finds itself in a much stronger position than when Steve took over in 2008, and the record of a league championship and three play-off appearances will be hard to match."

The second key action was for the new consortium to secure manager Alan Dowson on a full-time contract, the first time Hampton had ever engaged a manager on such a basis. The message was clear: Hampton were going to go for promotion next season.

National League South: 2017/18 Season

New season, new regime and the usual shuffling of the playing squad. Whilst the overall budget did not see a significant increase, manager Alan Dowson had the reassurance that the funding was in place to see out the season without the uncertainties that had beset previous seasons. The aim was to retain the core of the squad but Dowson felt changes were needed at centre back which had caused him a few headaches so it was farewell to club captain Kieran Murphy, Joe Hicks and Jay Gasson and hello to Charlie Wassmer who joined from Maidenhead, Claudiu Vilcu from Wingate & Finchley and youngster Jack Cook from Worthing. Vilcu, however, did not last long after an error strewn league debut at East Thurrock and Cook was promoted to become Wassmer's regular partner.

Also departing was Harold Odametey who was snapped up by newly promoted Maidenhead Utd and so Dowson brought in former Beaver Shaun McAuley who had last played under Alan Devonshire and now assumed the role of midfield anchor. Attacking options were strengthened with Woking's Max Kretzschmar, Welling's Harry Crawford, another former Beaver Ryan Moss, and wide attacker Taurean Roberts from Tooting & Mitcham. Moss had not particularly endeared himself to supporters on his previous stay five years earlier and once again failed to produce much in the way of goals with just two in 13 appearances. Crawford similarly flattered to deceive and having been signed on a long term contract spent most of the season on the bench or injured. For goals Hampton looked somewhat reliant on former Wycombe striker Kretzschmar who was a natural finisher although not an out and out centre forward.

Roberts was also another signing that quickly fell out of favour and with Duncan Culley mostly injured and out of form Hampton did start to look short of goals.

It was Kretzschmar who got the only goal in the held over Middlesex Senior Cup final against Wealdstone played at the Beveree, but more significantly, Wassmer's red card after an off the ball incident meant that he would be suspended for the first three league games, Nathan Collier drafted to fill his place. Defensive solidity was not however the issue as the league season got underway with a series of low scoring games in which Hampton managed just four goals in the first seven fixtures, only two of those scored by attacking players. One win in eight left Hampton in a disappointing 15th place, not the start the new regime had hoped for or expected. Yet another red card for Wassmer in the 2-2 draw with Dartford led to a five game suspension and many wondering whether the defender had a long term future at the club. Dowson, who was a known disciplinarian, decided to stick with Wassmer whose commanding presence was to become a decisive factor as the season progressed. The next five games brought a run of frustrating draws including a 1-1 home draw against lowly Potters Bar Town in the FA Cup 2nd Qualifying Round where the Beavers were bailed out by a late Duncan Culley penalty, Brendan Kiernan having missed one earlier. It was to prove Culley's last game before moving to Hayes & Yeading.

Dowson was never one slow to ring the changes. One of the expected benefits of his full-time role was the ability to watch games at clubs higher up the pyramid where he might be able to negotiate loan deals for players needing more game time or the challenge of more than U23 football. Dowson formed good working connections at Oxford Utd, Barnet and Sutton Utd which saw the likes of Bradley Hudson-Odoi, Malachi Napa, Adam Coombes, Dan Sweeney, Sam Long and Shandon Baptiste all come in for various successful spells. Dowson had attracted plenty of criticism in the past for a revolving door of loanees who often failed to have an impact but this time his choices seemed to hit the mark, the only trouble being the need to hand them back just when they were hitting form. Sam Howes was another case in point, having moved from West Ham to Watford over the close season, Dowson managed to persuade Watford to loan Howes back out until the end of the year and he played all but one game in that time. The back five of Howes, Casey, Wassmer, Cook and Kamara or Collier played in the majority of games and formed a solid unit but once Howes was recalled by his parent club Dowson was forced to cycle through a number of short term replacements until he lucked out with the loan signing of QPR's Seny Dieng.

It took a while for the changes to gel. Patience ran out with Ryan Moss after a near miss in the FA Cup against lower league opposition, Cinderford Town. Second half substitute, Brendan Kiernan, bailed out his team with a brace of goals to come from behind to avoid another unwelcome giant killing of the Taunton variety. Hampton then failed to progress any further in a home tie against a strong Truro City side despite having won a point away at their place just the Saturday before. As they say, Hampton now concentrated on the league and an upswing in form co-incided with the arrival on loan of midfielder Dan Sweeney from Barnet, another of Dowson's former Kingstonian protégées. Still in 15th place Hampton started to put together a run of form which saw eight consecutive league wins and a total of 10 victories on the bounce lifting them up to 3rd place equal on 38 points with Dartford and Braintree Town. The league was in fact a very close-run thing with just seven points covering the top 11 clubs so going into the second half of the season everything was up for grabs. With striker Adam Coombes returned to parent club Sutton Utd and Hudson-Odoi loaned out to Eastleigh, Dowson was back on the hunt for someone to lead the line and brought in well-travelled front man Elliot Charles from Ware Town and Shaun Jeffers on loan from National League Boreham Wood. It wasn't to be a long term career move for Charles, not known for being that prolific in front of goal, but he will go down in Hampton annals as the scorer of a thirteen minute hattrick away at Wealdstone in the New Year's Day fixture which stretched the unbeaten streak to 18 games. That record was then extended to 21 games before ending with a 2-0 away defeat by Bath City leaving Hampton still handily placed in second behind leaders Dartford with Havant & Waterlooville closing in with games in hand. A disappointing draw at home to last place Whitehawk followed but with Dartford losing to Chelmsford it meant that Hampton could go top if they won their game in hand. Instead, it was another draw at lowly Chippenham Town this time Shaun Jeffers' 95th minute header rescuing a point.

Jeffers was again on late goal duty scoring an 85th minute winner in a narrow home win over lowly Bognor Regis Town and followed up with another goal in the 3-1 win over Weston-super-Mare, the two other goals coming from Hudson-Odoi who had now signed for Hampton on a permanent basis. In the meantime, Havant had pushed on relentlessly winning their games in hand and topped the table by the time Hampton came to play them away in mid-March. The 0-0 draw was hard fought with the result better suiting Havant who had opened up a five point lead with Hampton now in third. With nine games to play Havant looked favourites for the one automatic promotion spot but with the play offs once again extending down to 7th place Hampton seemed very comfortably placed for one of the six play-off berths if they could not overhaul Havant. The question then became, where was the best place to finish as second and third places were spared participation in the first round of sudden death play-off games and given home advantage in the semi-finals.

The run in prove to be as nerve-wracking as ever as Hampton began to slip vital points against Braintree Town, Welling Utd, Concord Rangers, Dartford and Gloucester City. In the penultimate game away at St Albans City, themselves chasing a play-off place in 6th, Hampton just needed a win to make sure they would finish in the top seven. Goals from Wassmer, Jeffers and Roberts secured the win leaving just the last home game to see out against Truro City who like St Albans were also in contention for the play offs. A 1-1 draw courtesy of a rare Jack Cook goal meant that Hampton finished 4th and Truro 7th bringing Truro back to the Beveree for the first play-off game the following Wednesday. It was the fourth time Hampton had played Truro in the season but without a win in the three previous meetings.

The play off turned out to be no less of a tight game following the pattern of the league match with Truro taking an early lead only to be pegged back by another Jack Cook equaliser. The second half saw Hampton ride their luck with Truro hitting the bar and then failing to convert a penalty, Dieng pulling off a brilliant save to parry the ball away to safety. Despite good chances for both sides the match went to extra time before substitute Hudson-Odoi grabbed two goals to see the Beavers through 3-1 and a semi-final the following Sunday away at Chelmsford City.

The extra time against Truro must have left a good few tired legs for the trip to Essex as Hampton struggled to get their game going in the first half with Chelmsford having the better chances and Hampton barely registering an attempt on goal. Dowson, never one to hide from voicing an opinion, gave his side the half-time hair-drier treatment and sent them back out to finish the job they had failed to start.

The game turned in the 53rd minute. Following a goal line melee from a Hampton corner Chelmsford's Barnum-Bobb was adjudged to have handled the ball on the line. The luckless Barnum-Bobb was red-carded and Max Kretzschmar kept his composure to score the vital goal and send Hampton through to their second play off final, this time to face Braintree Town, surprise winners over Dartford. Although Braintree had finished 6th Hampton had lost and drawn against them in the league fixtures and they were certainly the side who were coming into the play offs with the necessary momentum.

Hampton fans had been here before, home advantage and the favourites tag to win a play-off final. Over 3,100 supporters packed into the Beveree on a hot sunny Sunday afternoon. Things could not have started better when leading scorer Kretzschmar was on the mark after just 8 minutes with a close range finish to put Hampton ahead. There were no further goals until just before half time when former Beaver Dan Thompson now playing for Braintree sent in a cross met by Robbie Grant to head home for 1-1. The second half predictably became a tense affair with few chances for either side but the loss late on of penalty-taker Kretzschmar with a head injury was destined to have an impact on the game further down the line as the match went into extra time. In the first period both sides seemed to decide that this was the time to push home the advantage with a flurry of chances but to no avail. The second period reverted to the cagey pattern of the second half as tired legs started to weigh up whether it was best to take their chances in a penalty shoot-out. And this was the fate awaiting both sides as neither team could find the decisive goal after 120 minutes of nerve-jangling football.

With Kretzschmar unavailable, Shaun Jeffers was first up to score for the Beavers before Braintree's Billy Crook blazed his spot kick over the bar to give Hampton the early advantage. The euphoria was however short lived as Josh Casey's weak effort was saved and then Dan Thompson levelled for the Iron. Charles and Barrington kept their nerves as both converted their spot kicks to make it 2-2. Brendan Kiernan unfortunately did not and skied his effort over the bar before Josh Hill made it 3-2. Hudson-Odoi netted for 3-3 but the final penalty fell to Diaz Wright who struck his shot into the top corner for 4-3 and Braintree into the National League just one season after being relegated.

It was the finest of margins but a crushing blow nonetheless for Dowson, his team and the supporters after a magnificent effort throughout the season. Whereas the season before the play offs had felt like an unexpected bonus, this time it seemed manifest destiny that Hampton would gain promotion with one of the strongest sides ever produced at the club. Could Dowson go one better next year? The answer was yes but not quite how Hampton fans might have imagined it.

Dowson's post-match interview seemed to hint that he was considering his future but the dust had barely settled and the tears barely dried when the next day Dowson announced that he was joining Woking who had just been relegated from the National League.

Whilst it was known in the weeks before that Woking were interviewing for a new manager, it had been reported that they had concluded their process before the play off final took place although no announcement had been made. The truth it seemed was that they were waiting on the outcome of the Braintree game to see if their real favourite might become available. There are few secrets in non-league football, and it was known at the club that Woking had approached Dowson a couple of seasons previously, but he had decided keep faith with Hampton. No doubt Dowson had one eye on developments at Kingfield and it would have been an interesting question whether he would have gone should Hampton have won promotion leap-frogging Woking on their way into the National League.

"*I have had to make the hardest decision of my managerial career to leave the club I hold in the highest regard,*" said Dowson, "*My thoughts are constantly turning to the wonderful people attached to Hampton & Richmond Borough as well as the hundreds of loyal and supportive fans who have cheered myself and the players to a string of achievements in the last four seasons.*"

Quite why Woking felt the need to rush into an announcement is not known when a few days grace might have sweetened the pill for Hampton fans and saved Dowson from criticism (wrong as it turned out) that he had lined up the new role before the final had taken place. It was a very messy end to one of the best periods in the club's recent history and left Hampton fans wondering where they went from here, losing Dowson, assistant Martin Tyler and Academy Manager Ian Dyer in the space of 24 hours plus the strong likelihood that many of the squad would follow Dowson to Woking.

Once the passions had subsided and calmer reflections on what Dowson had achieved could take place, it was clear that this was one of the highpoints of Hampton's long history. First team coach Ian Dyer summed up Dowson's appeal quite succinctly:

"*He has an unbelievable ability to relate to everybody at the club, from the star striker to the tea lady. One of his biggest strengths is making everybody feel valued and a part of the team. He is always keen to help and support people within the local community and is very hands on and generous with his time. I'm not sure you'd find anybody that wouldn't admire what he has done for this football club.*"

Dowson came into the club with a reputation for wringing the last drop out of meagre playing budgets and for galvanising everyone involved with his infectious enthusiasm and constant drive to improve every aspect of the team. In the early days this sometime felt like a scatter-gun approach particularly with the high turnover of players in the first season and sometimes it was hard to see the wood for the trees. This was partly due to arriving mid-way through the season and having to juggle a squad that badly needed trimming and having to recruit players who by definition should already have regular places elsewhere. Once Dowson had a pre-season to plan with, his squads settled down and he put his faith in a core of players who responded to his challenge. Undoubtedly Hampton fans saw a much better team in Dowson's final season than the budget really deserved. In Lowe and Kabamba, Diarra and Odametey, Wassmer, Casey, Cook , Kiernan and Kretzschmar he found top quality players who showed that they were capable of playing at a higher level and supplemented these with judicious loan signings such as Howes, Dieng, Baptiste and Long. His record was pretty much the same as Alan Devonshire's with promotions and play off finals. The club was indeed fortunate to have had both as managers.

Manager's Record

	P	W	D	L	F	A	Pts	Ave	Win%
Alan DOWSON									
Combined	213	103	53	57	384	256			48.4
League	167	79	49	39	293	199	286	1.71	47.3
Play Offs	5	2	0	3	7	6			
Cup	41	22	4	15	84	51			53.6

The Hampton and Richmond Borough Football Family

The Demise of Reserve Team Football

The Beavers always used to have a Reserve Team playing in a competitive league of other club's second teams. Known under various, sometimes 'derogatory terms' as 'The Stiffs', 'Seconds', 'A's' or just 'the Ressies'.

Clubs used the reserves in several ways: somewhere to bring back injured players to match fitness; as a bridge between Youth and Adult football; or to keep 'Squad' players in football, if they weren't guaranteed a game for the first team.

Usually competing in a regional league, to cut travelling costs, matches were quite often played in front of sparse crowds with little information available as to who was out there playing for the club. Indeed, it was a struggle often to get anyone to collect an admission fee, provide hot drinks or even open up the club house for spectators.

Teams playing under the Hampton banner competed in various leagues, usually connected in some way with the parent league that the first team were members of. When Hampton joined the Spartan League, it had its own reserve league run for its member clubs. As Hampton progressed up the Football Pyramid, they were long time members of the Suburban Football League, formed in 1971, who provided reserve team football for clubs who were members of various South-East leagues (Isthmian/Combined Counties etc). The league was generally split into three Divisions: a Premier Division, a North Division and a South Division. There was therefore scope for promotion and relegation, though given the nature of the differing make-up of a team from one game to another, let alone from one season to another, this was really only to provide some form of competitive edge to the contests.

The Suburban League also ran various cup competitions to supplement their league programme and it was also possible for clubs to enter the Middlesex Premier Cup, which mixed reserve teams and what we might call 'park football' teams.

The Beavers finally left the realms of reserve team football and last competed in the Suburban League in 2014/15 having also had a brief dalliance with the Capital Football League, which was touted as mainly a midweek league.

There are many reasons why the club quit second team football which include saving wear and tear on the pitch, saving money and also removing a level of team management (not forgetting the physio). Less use of floodlights for late afternoon and evening matches, reduction in amount of kit needed, match official's expenses etc are all used as arguments against a reserve team.

Nowadays it is easier to loan out players to other clubs or arrange the occasional friendly to give players 'game time'. What is missing though is the lack of a 'step-up' from youth to senior football. However, the Academy system now goes some way to alleviating that problem although not without its critics. The Suburban League is still in existence but is now populated with Under 23 and Under 21 teams. The Beavers do have the capacity to re-enter the competition if there is the will and finance to do so – whether that will happen remains to be seen.

During the period of this history, Reserve team football can best be described as sporadic. After a number of years without a reserve team, a side managed by Mike Howe took part in the Suburban League South in 2004/05 (finishing 6th). But it was then disbanded until revived in 2008/09 under Andy Cook (5th place).

The Reserves switched to the North division for next season under Mark Harper and were crowned Champions, 2009/10, gaining promotion to the Premier Division. The following year, now under the leadership of Andy Smith, the Ressies finished a creditable 3rd. As we have seen Mark Harper went on to become first team manager and the same route was followed by Paul Barry who had taken over for the 2011/12 season.

It was decided to introduce a midweek side into the Under 23 competition, the Capital League, in 2012/13 but this and the regular Reserves side fell foul of the financial constraints and all second team football was abandoned after 2014/15.

The costs versus benefits were frequently debated particularly given the gulf between Academy and First Team standards. Good Academy players it was argued were being lost to the club as they had nowhere within the Beveree set up to make the transition to "men's" football. This was undoubtedly true but facing the cost of maintaining this infrastructure as opposed to working with other non-league sides to farm out promising talent seemed to be the more efficient option. Whether these were viewed as loans or permanent signings is neither here nor there. Such is the fluidity of non-league football; players are very much used to moving around a number of clubs to gain experience and opportunity.

It is a feature of the game these days that many clubs use the loan system to maximise their squads whilst reducing the cost of talent. League clubs want their players to experience meaningful matches with the higher physical demands available at non-league level and seem happy to foot the bill. Getting a young full time player who may be on £500-1,000 per week at a pro club frees up a significant amount of budget to spend elsewhere. Similarly, nonleague clubs can help place their promising youth and Academy players with clubs where they can keep an eye on progress with a view to bringing them back at some later stage. But in practice, as managers change the continuity is lost and Hampton rarely benefited from this strategy.

The overall rise in the number professional club academies has also meant that there are now many more players being processed through the system, and certainly many more than there are places in the professional first and reserve teams. This releases a large number of players into the non-league system and club managers are never short of agents or players looking for trials. And so, the relevance of the Reserve team has declined. Those clubs that maintain a presence in reserve football very much focus on the U23 development side of the game as a bridge for their academies.

The Rise of The Football Academy

In the dim and distant past if you were young and wanted to be a professional footballer, you needed to have talent (obviously) and the luck to be seen by a scout attached to a Football Club. If you impressed at a trial then the aspiring player would sign on as an apprentice and his football education would start.

Sweeping terraces, tidying up after a game, scrubbing out the dressing rooms and worst of all cleaning a first team player's boots – that was the sum total of the 'education'. Some players, of their own volition carried on studies at college or night school. The apprentice would, if he was lucky, get game time with the Reserves or a 'A' team. If the lucky individual made it then he would be signed on, if not he would be discarded and possibly drop down into what we now call Non-League football, possibly having wasted several years of his life with no qualifications to help get employment outside the football factory.

That all changed in the late 1990s with the Football Association's 'Charter of Quality' introduced by Howard Wilkinson. In general clubs can sign players aged 9 – 16 on a schoolboy contract. After the age of 16 players can be offered a place on their Youth Training Scheme allowing them to combine football training with educational studies. The Football Academy later spread to Non-League Clubs in conjunction with companies set up to promulgate the needs of young players. Hampton started its Academy for Under 19s in 2010/11 (having had an Under 18 team playing in a midweek league for many years).

Pre Academy

Youth teams have been a feature of the club since becoming a Senior club in 1959. Various age-related teams playing in a variety of local leagues have been recorded in match day programmes. In the recent past (despite one or two minor changes) the focus was on midweek football for Under 18s played under the auspices of initially the Southern Youth League which morphed into the Isthmian Youth League – though membership is not entirely limited to Isthmian League teams. Divisions are split geographically with play-offs at the end of the season to decide the overall Champions. There is also the facility for a League Cup and, of course, the Middlesex FA Youth Cup.

Youth team celebrates Middlesex Senior Youth Cup

Youth teams tend to be cyclical, because players would only be eligible for, probably, two years, and teams were always bringing in new younger players at the bottom as older players departed at the top end. The strength, or not, of a youth team could change from year to year, largely depending on the intake. Occasionally a youth team would gel into a winning unit, as in 2017/18. On March 7th 2018 the Under 18 side made it through to the Middlesex Senior Youth Cup Final at Uxbridge against Bedfont Sports in front of a crowd of just under 200. After going 1-0 down early in the second half, they fought back to win 3-1 with two goals from Pierre Moulin and one from Shadraq Malembe. This was first time that a Hampton team had won the Senior Youth Cup (in the side was Imran Uche who later returned in 2020 to stake a first team place).

The Academy

Starting in 2010/11, the club now run an Under 19 Academy side in conjunction with its Under 18 team. The Under 18s continuing to ply their trade on midweek evenings at Beveree under floodlights, the Under 19s, usually on a Wednesday afternoon, at Hanworth Villa, though they previously played at a local Sports and Leisure complex.

Steve Bates, Academy Manager

From small beginnings the Under 19 competition has grown to 11 divisions, including two Elite Divisions, and the number of teams competing to 121. The Academy team competed in the Football Conference Youth League which included Boreham Wood, Kingstonian, Tottenham Hotspur and Woking amongst others. In that first season, the Academy team finished in mid table and Dan Thompson made a few appearances for the first team. The first Academy Manager was Peter Augustine, a qualified football coach.

Hampton's Academy team is now playing at the Elite level, against what is arguably a very strong coterie of clubs which include Sutton United and Maidenhead United.

After a number of years, Peter moved on to be replaced by Koo Dumbaya, and then by Ian Dyer who was also coaching the First XI under Alan Dowson. The appointment of Dyer gave a boost to the Academy as Dowson's club-wide philosophy made him open to giving an opportunity for the best players to train with the First XI and get game time mainly in the minor cup competitions. This proactive view of the Academy has continued under the guidance of current Academy manager, Steve Bates, and first team manager, Gary McCann.

Peter Augustine summed up the viewpoint in an interview in 2015:

"It is extremely important for there to be a clear pathway in to the first team for these boys," he said. *" Without that we are offering, nothing to these boys. When Alan [Dowson] arrived at the club he told the boys he would be looking at them and pushing them into the reserves and then the first team. That does not change just because he has signed one or two players."*

He added: *"Since I have been at the club, we have had at least one boy play in the first team, but they have only made one, two or three appearances. We need to start producing players who play and start 15 games a season for the first team and we are getting close to that point where we are producing players of that quality on a regular basis."*

A number of players have come through the club's Academy programme to make appearances in the first team. Dan Thompson, Paris Mason and Charlie ten Grotenhuis and George Wells all came through the Academy. Imran Uche, after a period playing at Bedfont has also returned to become a regular member of the First XI under Gary McCann with Jamie Hope and Joe Wotton also on the fringes in recent sesons. It would be fair to say that the club would have liked to see more boys progressing, but such is the competition from League clubs for local talent it is hard for smaller non-league academies to attract the best players. Facilities remain a constraint compared to the luxury of league clubs. The club has looked at investing more funds into improving classroom space over the years, but the economics have been hard to make work.

Imran Uche, one of the Academy players now a regular in the First XI

Of course, not every student has the ability or desire to play senior football but the education side to the Academy is just as important. They come away with a useful qualification and development of the individual, as a fully rounded person is regarded just as important as success on the pitch. The Academy's students are also encouraged to be a part of the community and take part in supporting a local charity. Covid-19 brought the' 2019/20 season to a full stop and during November 2020 there was a suspension of football, before re-starting in December. The Academy still planned for normality to return and started to look forward to welcoming the next intake, hopefully in more normal conditions.

The education portion of the Academy continued in line with the Government's wish to see schools/colleges and universities stay open. Season 2020/21 saw a late September start to the Academy fixtures but by November the season went into suspension, as did the Under 18s, as Covid-19 brought a stop to all football below National League South/North.

With another lockdown in force Academy Students were having to study from home. Zoom meetings with parents and the boys became the norm for them as with other educational and sporting establishments.

Unexpectedly, the option for a return came as the Government's Four Step Roadmap kicked in and, educationally at least, the students returned on Monday 8th March 2021 to their classroom at Beveree. A chink of light then appeared with the opportunity of competitive football as well. The Middlesex Football Association announced that they had drawn the Quarter Finals of the 2020/21 Middlesex Senior Cup competition. Hampton were drawn at home to Spelthorne Sports (Combined Counties League) to be played in mid-April. Because all senior players were on furlough, the only team that could fulfil the fixture was the Academy. Having had no competitive football since November 4th, some five months earlier, it seemed that the Academy boys would be partaking of a First Team fixture with the possibility of a Semi-Final and even a Cup Final later in the spring.

The Academy lost the game 4-0 so there was no question of any further progression but they acquitted themselves with honour. Some of the squad have since gone on to feature in the 2021/22 pre season.

The Revival of Women's Football

Hampton have, on and off, had a women's team since 1997, originally playing in the South East Counties League before graduating to the Greater London Women's Football League (GLWFL). On occasions, the team have graced the Beveree pitch and at other times played home games on neighbouring sports pitches. It is fair to say that not all of Hampton's Club Officials have seen the benefits of having a Women's team. This attitude did not sit well with the Club's aim of being a Community Club.

Women's Football is not something that has recently sprung out of equality and diversity, it has a history of its own that goes back to the First World War. Around the time of the First World War, women's football was big news, with millions of men serving the colours, women suddenly became the factory workers and breadwinners. Women's football teams sprang up, linked to factories, and, starved of sporting entertainment, thousands flocked to professional grounds to watch their matches.

When peace broke out in 1918 how did the Football Association react? The FA banned women from playing on club grounds. The women were sent back, in the main to where they were thought to belong, back to marriage, mothering and to domestic duties leaving women's football to become a minority interest in this country. It was not until 1993 that the FA finally established a Women's Football Committee – female football was, once again, mainstream.

Hampton currently has a team in the Greater London Women's League (GLWL) which sits at Level 7 to 9 in the Women's FA Pyramid, playing in the Premier Division (level 7) their highest level to date. The next step up would be to the London & South East Women's Regional Football League, Level 6. Just like

Dick Kerr's Ladies playing in front of full grounds

the Men's Pyramid there have been numerous changes and re-alignments to leagues and levels over the years, which make tracking back notoriously difficult.

The Women's team were originally formed as Brentford & Hampton Ladies FC, and they started to play regularly at Beveree during the 1996/97 season in front of crowds of between 30 and 70. In 1997/98 the Brentford tag was dropped, and Hampton Ladies won the GLWL championship, securing the Premier Division title at Beveree with a 5-0 thrashing of QPR Ladies in front of an attendance of 62. At one time their manager was none other than Alan Devonshire, who started out in management at Osterley FC as well as managing Brentford and Osterley Ladies which then morphed into Hampton Ladies.

Hampton Ladies became very much part of the club, even organising a Charity Parachute jump during the summer of 1998 at Hinton-in-the-Hedges in Northamptonshire, included were a number of supporters willing to risk life and limb. At the end of each season a match to raise funds for charities such as the Shooting Star Trust between the Ladies and a team made up of supporters would regularly take place.

At the beginning of the 2002/03 season, it was announced that a new incarnation of the Women's team, playing as Hampton and Richmond Borough Women would be starting life in the Greater London League (GLR) – Division 4 West. The team was not directly part of the club but run as a separately funded operation by some members of the main club committee.

Hampton Women, playing at Beveree, the team were in Division 1 by 2004/05. At the beginning of the 2006/07 season, it was accepted that the Women's team would be playing at Beveree, however there seemed to be a change of policy. Perhaps affected by having homeless Feltham FC play matches at Beveree, and to prevent problems with preparing the pitch, the decision was made to ask the Women's team to play off-site, which they have continued to do until the present time. It is fair to say that the Ladies Team were not treated particularly well at this time by the main club board and confusion reigned about how the club wanted to engage.

The decision to prevent Sunday afternoon football at Beveree meant that in many respects the members of the team felt distanced from the main club, despite carrying the club's name. Regardless of playing away from Beveree, results and fixtures form part of the Hampton Match Day programme.

In 2014/15 the team won GLWFL Division 2(South). Currently, the team play at Tudor Park Sports and Leisure in Feltham. During season 2019/20 the women were given the opportunity to once again play at Beveree, under lights, taking part in a regional cup competition. A crowd of 75 turned up to watch Hampton beat Woking Ladies 5-4 (after extra time) – even ex-Hampton Manager, Alan Dowson came along to watch. Unfortunately, with the suspension of the season there was no further opportunity for taking part in the next round.

At the start of the 2020/21 season, they were promoted from Division One to the Premier Division of the GLWFL. The season had hardly got under way than it was brought to a halt by Covid-19 and various lockdowns. All football below National League South/North being suspended, which took account of all 'grassroots' football. When season 2020/21 ended the team found themselves at the foot of the table after 9 games. There would appear to be little chance of the Women's team taking the field again until season 2021/22.

Louise Clark celebrates scoring the goal that secured top spot

Unfortunately, the Ladies team have recently disbanded, with the Youth Section taking on the mantle of providing Women's Football. There are two girl's teams competing under the Hampton Youth banner in the Surrey County Women's and Girls Football League. Before the cessation of the season the two teams played on a side pitch at Hanworth Villa, however a request was made to the London Borough of Richmond for an additional small-sided pitch to be marked out on Hampton Common, which would enable the teams to play 'in Borough' rather than in the London Borough of Hounslow. Needless to say, permission has been delayed by Covid-19.

Pan Disability

What is pan-disability football? A very good question! It would seem that the Football Association have taken on board that diversity in football is a good thing. Gradually, the football authorities have moved beyond the Men's Game into Women's Football – after banning it in the 1920s - and into football for the disabled (in its many forms, seen and unseen). There are many strands of football that may to some extent remain under the radar like Deaf Football and a more recent development like, Pan-Disability Football. Just like the Football Pyramid there are various levels of this part of the sport. The FA now see it as part of their remit to provide football for those formerly excluded from sport by virtue of their special needs and disabilities. The intention is to provide football for players with any type of disability or mental health problem.

Hampton has its own Pan-Disability team in which Bill Glassop and his son, James, our dedicated Kit Managers play a major role. The link between Pan-Disability and Hampton is relatively recent however, those involved have been connected with this aspect of the game since at least 2000. James has played in

Back row l to r: Michael Thomas, Jack Scott, Josh Brunskill, Darren Blair, James Glassup, Daniel James

Front row l to r: Alec Barry, Saif Alani, Senol Kasim, Antony Barnett, Jay Cash. Photo Bill Glassup

disability football for over 20 years and always hoped that, one day, he would be able to represent the Beavers.

In 2014, David Sines, the Vice- Chairman at the time, asked James to set up a team to represent the club. In the early years there were only a handful of clubs taking part and in order to take part in competitions long trips were the order of the day, even as far away as Northampton. Currently the situation is very much improved, both the Middlesex FA and the Surrey FA now have officials dedicated to the disabled footballers through what is known as the initiative *Football For All*. A lot of the work on the ground is, you won't be surprised to hear, still done by volunteers.

Hampton Pan-Disability take part under the auspices of the Surrey FA. The League has four Adult Divisions (Premier, Championship, League 1 & League 2) and 3 Junior Divisions (U16 Premiership, U16 Championship and U12s), catering for all levels of ability.

Fixtures are held once a month, with teams competing across Surrey and the South East. As a mark of its success the League won the 2020 Grassroots League of the Year at Surrey FA's Grassroots Football Awards. In the inaugural season Hampton Pan-Disability were allocated to the Championship Division, which they duly won to gain promotion to the Premiership at the first attempt. A measure of their performances was the 8-2 win over Clarendon Youth Club in their first ever game. In 2015 the team finished 3rd and continue to play at the Premiership level to this day. Many of the original team are still playing together.

There is also the opportunity to play in a FA National competition that starts at a local level with the chance to progress through Regional Finals.

In 2018 Hampton Pan-Disability, won their way through tournaments in Kent & Sussex (thank goodness for the club Mini-Bus!), beating established teams like Southampton FC, to get to the South East Finals, held at Slough Town's Arbour Park. Hampton's opponents consisted of Northampton Town, MK Dons and the hosts, Slough Town. Despite being unsuccessful on the day, being one of the top four teams in the South East of England was a massive achievement for which the players (and management) should be very proud. In 2019 Hampton Pan-Disability were once again at Arbour Park in the Semi-Finals just missing out on a Final on goal difference.

2020 and 2021 has, of course, brought its own problems when you take into consideration the effect that Covid-19 can have on those with various health problems. Grassroots Football at all levels has been affected by the pandemic but it is so important that those with underlying health issues take even greater care to stay safe.

Training would normally take place once a week and they would also have been playing in a 5-a-side league, but currently it is all on hold. Just like all those involved in sport, at any level, our Hampton Pan-Disability Team cannot wait to get out on that pitch again.

The last word on the subject should be left to one of the original team members, Alec Barry........

"Having a Pan-Disability team means a lot to me as someone who couldn't cut the mustard in adult competitive football, it's nice to have a new way to be able to pull on the famous Red & Blue, as opposed to wheeling round the garden pretending to be Charlie Moone."

"It has been a massive help with my mental health, knowing that I have a reason to leave the house on a Sunday morning. We may not be world beaters, but I have a great (mostly) time being out there."

"Representing Hampton is a feeling I can't put into words really, yes, I know it's not the real deal and I'm not in Gary's starting XI, but it means just the same as if I was. I almost carry a weight of expectation with me once I'm kitted out and laced up on Sunday morning."

Hampton & Richmond Borough Youth

The youth are the future footballers of tomorrow and just as importantly ……….the supporters of tomorrow; ignore them at your peril!

Currently HRBFC has very strong links with Youth Football. HRBFC Youth section is closely linked with the main club, playing in the colours of the club and carrying the name of the main club in several local Youth Leagues. There have always been a number of youth teams in and around Hampton. Hampton Rangers and Hampton Youth being two of the oldest youth teams. There have been numerous other teams, some being short-lived including Hampton Harriers, Hampton Thistle, Hampton Manor, Hampton Diamonds & Hampton Wanderers (this list is not exhaustive). Mostly playing in the Surrey Youth League – which used to be called the West Surrey Boys League – there are now both boys and girl's teams competing at all age groups.

The two main 'rivals' for recruiting youngster to play youth football have traditionally been Hampton Rangers & Hampton Youth.

HRBFC Under 13s

Hampton Rangers are based in Oldfield Road, Hampton, and have their own ground and pitches on site and also uses pitches on Hatherop Recreation Ground – where Hampton FC played for many years leading up to 1959.

Hampton Youth hosted matches at many venues and used to have changing rooms on Buckingham Fields, Buckingham Road in Hampton (now called Hampton Common). Sadly, their building fell into disrepair thanks to frequent attacks of vandalism and had to be pulled down.

One former graduate of Hampton Youth was Jim Wigmore who came to Hampton FC in 1980 and made 244 appearances for the Beavers.

On 20th December 2008, during the half time interval of the home game with Basingstoke Town a new Juniors section was introduced to the supporters. HRBFC Juniors had 10 teams from Under 12s to Under 16s in two leagues (Surrey Youth & Tandridge Youth Leagues). The teams were formerly part of Tooting & Mitcham United and were now part of HRBFC (though for F A reasons those teams would still have to complete the season under the T & M name).

Having dipped its toe into organising its own Youth Section, negotiations commenced with Hampton Youth in order to bring the two youth football clubs under the single banner of HRBFC. The organisers of Hampton Youth agreed in principle to merge the two clubs. In 2012/13 Hampton Youth adopted HRBFC as part of its name, and by 2015/16 the full change of name to HRBFC Youth had taken place.

HRBFC Youth has expanded the number of teams (including girl's teams). The club is represented by 34 teams and is competing in Saturday (East Berkshire Alliance) and Sunday

Football (Surrey Youth League, Surrey Primary League and Surrey Girls & Women League). The age range for the youngsters now go from U7 to U18s, (training starts from U5s).

Due to the number of teams involved teams are now playing matches at many venues, some out of Borough; Bushey Park, Hampton Common, St Pauls School, Sunbury and Hanworth Villa are all currently used. Unfortunately, the pitches at Kingsfield were lost to the club after the landlords made an agreement with Harlequins Rugby Club. The club are in ongoing discussion with Richmond Council in order to increase the availability of pitches in our own local area.

HRBFC Youth are self-funding, relying on membership/match fees to operate. The main expenditure being on pitch fees and kit and equipment. HRBFC Youth are fully compliant with the Football Association's guidance with reference to Safeguarding and are a well-respected youth club within their respective leagues. HRBFC maintain a good relationship with the main club and the aim is that there is a pathway for youngsters to join the club and progress up through the age groups into Under 18/Academy Football.

The McCann Years: 2018-21

National League South: 2018/19 Season

As many feared, skipper Josh Casey, Jack Cook, Christian Jolley, Michael Kamara, Brendan Kiernan, Max Kretzschmar and Charlie Wassmer all followed Alan Dowson out of the club with most taking the short trip to Woking. Given the fact that most of the remaining first team players were loanees, there would be precious little left for any incoming manager to work with. The search was on.

With little time to waste an early appointment was made on 24th May. The man chosen was Ryman Premier Hendon's Manager, Gary McCann. The appointment was popular as McCann's name had been on many supporters' lips.

Chris Dickson

Gary McCann

45 year old Gary McCann had become an institution at Hendon, first joining them in 1997 as a goalkeeper, making 196 appearances before taking on the manager's role in 2005. Having lost their ground, it had been a difficult few years for the club but McCann showed loyalty beyond the call of duty when he might have easily moved on for an easier life. Just like the Beavers, McCann's Hendon had fallen short at the play off stage in a penalty shoot-out just a few weeks earlier but now found that he had, in fact, a different route into the National League South. Looking for a new challenge, he decided the time was right to step into the vacant Hampton hot seat. Chairman Graham Wood was able to maintain the playing budget enjoyed by Alan Dowson.

It really was a case of starting from scratch, recruiting a whole new squad and backroom team. The situation was partially resolved by bringing along the entire Hendon management team plus a number of players that he knew well: Rian Bray, Michael Corcoran, Zak Joseph, Tom Lovelock, Casey MacLaren, Josh McLeod-Urquhart, Jake Eggleton, James Hammond and Daniel Uchechi all followed McCann (recalling the time that Alan Devonshire brought almost an entire squad from Maidenhead United to the Beavers). But it wasn't just Hendon re-branded as Hampton. McCann brought in two experienced players from Wealdstone,

Ricky Wellard, who was made captain and midfielder Matty Wichelow. Up front he signed Chris Dickson, a player with league experience at Gillingham and such non-league sides as Chelmsford City. Also signing was Craig Dundas from Sutton Utd, back after a seven year absence for his second spell at the club. Wide attacker Rhys Murrell-Williamson, voted into the team of the season for 2017/18, joined from St Albans City whilst the versatile Tyrell Miller-Rodney made the short trip up the Thames from Staines Town. Dan Bowry, a centre back was brought in on a six month loan from Leyton Orient. Left back Nathan Mavila, previously at West Ham and Leyton Orient was a late addition. Only Taurean Roberts remained from the previous season's squad but departed after only a couple of games, McCann being well covered for that attacking wing position.

Ten players made their debut in the first League match, a 1-1 draw away to newly promoted Slough Town which was a steady, if unspectacular start. It took just 3 minutes for Zak Joseph to open his goalscoring account but Slough equalised mid-way through the half and probably had the best of the rest of the game. This was followed by a couple of narrow defeats and then a first win away at St Albans City, 3-2, one of the goals a spectacular overhead bicycle kick from Casey Maclaren. Some added experience at the back was needed as Bowry wasn't quite cutting the mustard and his loan was terminated. McCann brought in the veteran Sutton Utd defender, Simon Downer. His previous injury record meant that he had to be used sparingly but when he played Hampton were noticeably tighter at the back. More encouragement was to follow when an away win at promotion favourites Torquay United (2-0) was quickly built on with another four wins (including another win at Torquay's Plainmoor ground – but this time against ground sharing Truro City). The wins boosted the league position from 18th to 3rd tucking in nicely behind big spending Billericay Town and Alan Dowson's Woking who were early pace setters. With Dickson scoring freely, the start had been much better than anyone could have expected. Good progress was also made in the initial rounds of the FA Cup, the Beavers easing their way past Burgess Hill Town (3-0), AFC Hornchurch (1-0) and an unexpected win at National League Premier Side, Eastleigh (1-0) – Dickson scoring the only goal of the game turning the tables over the home favourites after a spirited Beavers' display. Hampton went into the First Round Proper for only the third time in their history, the draw giving them a home draw against Oldham Athletic from EFL2. Oldham were not without their problems in the league and a giant killing was not beyond expectation. The tie would have been an attraction in itself but then the game was switched to be the live FA Cup game on BT Sports – not only that but BBC decided that the club would also host the live draw for the 2nd Round of the F A Cup at 7pm the same evening. As far as the club was aware this would be the first time that two Television Companies would be providing simultaneous live transmissions from a Non-League club.

Whether the FA Cup game would distract the players was a very good question. The answer seemed "yes" as the run up to the tie saw League form start to dip with no wins in five beforehand, dropping Hampton back to 16th place. Hampton were developing a worrying habit of conceding very early goals having gone behind within six minutes in four out of the last five league games. It almost felt that they needed to give a goal away before they could knuckle down to play football. After the 4-2 home defeat by Oxford City, Gary McCann was candid in his assessment:

"First half from hell. I am really disappointed with the result today. There are clearly minds that are elsewhere as the level of performance in the last three games since the Eastleigh win have not been good enough."

"There are no guaranteed places for that game now and that is very much down to performance and if they think they are guaranteed a place then they are kidding themselves, me and the club."

There was just three weeks between the draw and the hosting of the game. It goes without saying that the Beavers were faced with a mountain of work to get the game on, not least the arrangements that had to be made for the Broadcasting Media, as well as other interested parties including the Emergency Services. The match was made all-ticket with segregation in place for the visitors, which involved the installation of a turnstile block near the halfway line – plus bringing in additional catering and temporary toilets. On the night itself 2,720 made their way into Beveree to see Dickson open the scoring with a hotly disputed first half penalty[15], only for Oldham to hit back, very late in the game, with two goals. Hampton perhaps showed a bit of naivety by pushing for a late winner themselves and then being caught on the counter attack. All credit to the club for all their hard work and, in particular, the volunteers and supporters who turned up to make the game a very special occasion. Without doubt, the high point of the season.

Despite the spirited display against Oldham, the next league fixture at home to Dartford saw the Beavers' defence last until just the 14th minute before conceding the only goal of the game. It must have driven McCann to distraction.

---

[15] Tyrell Miller-Rodney who had won the penalty was later given a three game suspension for simulation. Trial by television indeed.

The Manager could count himself unlucky that injuries curtailed the appearances of some of his ex-Hendon cohort such as Casey MacLaren, Ollie Sprague and Michael Corcoran. Downer was never fit enough to be a regular and so McCann drafted in Yado Mambo shortly before the Oldham tie to play alongside Rian Bray. He resisted giving Mambo the No5 shirt much to supporters' disappointment! Mambo himself was coming back from a career threatening injury so was also a bit of a risk and didn't stay long in the side. Wealdstone midfielder Sam Cox then came in on loan (before being signed on a permanent basis) to shore up the midfield. Luke Ruddick, who could play right or centre back joined from Oxford City to give more defensive options. However, Craig Dundas re-joined Sutton Utd when they themselves had an injury crisis leaving the Beavers light up front at just the wrong time. He returned to see out the season a few weeks later.

McCann had stated at the start of the season that he was not a fan of using the loan market preferring to build a squad over time rather than see a revolving door of players come and go. Most supporters shared the same viewpoint. However, Alan Dowson had shown that with the right deals, loans could be beneficial and, in a world, where players barely lasted more than one season with a club, the concept of someone being a 'permanent' signing was perhaps running its course.

With gaps left by injury and loss of form McCann took the plunge and decided to dip into the loan market. Left back Jack Connors came in on loan from Dover Athletic and was considered a success, Richard Orlu from Welling and midfielder Liam Sole from MK Dons, less so. Wide attacker Ryan Hill also signed after having been released by Stoke City but with chances limited was sent out on loan to Egham to gain match fitness. To the end of the season the loan players kept rolling through with various levels of impact.

Goals became increasingly hard to come by. Chris Dickson's goalscoring form tailed off dramatically after the New Year with only five of his 19 goals scored after December. Dundas was less than prolific and often deployed in midfield rather than attack. The form of Joseph, Murrell-Williamson, Uchechi and others drafted in to bolster the line was inconsistent until the arrival of Leyton Orient loanee, Ruel Sotiriou, later in the season gave the forward line the shot in the arm it needed. His six goals in a handful of games made him third highest scorer behind Dickson and Joseph.

The winter holiday fixture list had decided the local derbies would be against 2nd placed Woking on Boxing and New Year's Day. The meeting of Hampton and 'Hampton Old Boys' was much anticipated. Of the 22 players on show, 18 had at some time or other played for the Beavers. Again, injury problems hampered the Beavers in the match at Kingfield with Ruddick, Sprague and Downer all unavailable. Craig Dundas was then pressed into an emergency central defender role after Corcoran broke down early in the first half. It finished 3-1 to Woking.

In the return game in front of a big Bank Holiday crowd at the Beveree, Hampton conceded in just the 4th minute and Woking looked rarely threatened as they won again easily 3-0. It was hard for Hampton supporters to see their old heroes handing out two straightforward defeats. The gulf between the two sides was very apparent and festive cheer was not the order of the day.

The New Year's resolution now was to stay in the division. Points were hard to come by, but just occasionally the team recovered its form, take the case of an away win at Oxford City (5-3) early in March then another away win at Billericay Town (3-1) at the beginning of April. The Billericay win was followed by victories over Wealdstone (2-1) and a comfortable away victory at relegation-bound Weston-super-Mare (2-0) which cemented safety before the final games of the season. The final position of 15th left Hampton 10 points above the drop zone. Their goals scored tally of 49 from 42 games was the 4th lowest in the league. Had it not been for the good early season form

Munira Wilson MP opens the newly refurbished terrace with chairman Jacques Le Bars and Vice chairman Ben Hudson

Hampton would have been in danger of dropping out the back door of the league. Six of the 13 league wins came in the first 10 games, just seven in the last 32. It was a tough learning curve for McCann but thankfully ended with the opportunity to go again the following season with league status intact.

Out of 52 games, Rian Bray made the most appearances, 47, followed by Keeper Tom Lovelock, 45 and Chris Dickson with 43. Dickson also led the scorers with 19, the second highest being Zak Joseph with just 8. 43 players trod the Beveree pitch during the season, showing the increased reliance on loan players – which as mentioned earlier went against McCann's preference.

Torquay United overcame their early season difficulties to finish as Champions by 10 points with Woking joining them in promotion via the play offs, beating Welling Utd 1-0 in the final, Alan Dowson putting to bed the hoodoo of the previous two seasons. Truro, East Thurrock and Weston super Mare were all relegated.

In the last home match programme of the season McCann made a point that the health of the squad had defined the season and that a full quota of players was essential for success in this league and that too often key players were out injured. Injuries to key players certainly played their part but it was equally apparent that some had failed to make the step up from Isthmian Premier level whilst others with more experience at Conference level were on a downward career trajectory. Building a side takes some time and in an unforgiving league time is not a luxury that is often afforded managers. It seemed quite likely that McCann would now have to shuffle the pack further for the coming season although not quite as he expected.

Off the pitch necessary improvements were needed to maintain the ground's B grading and a grant was secured from The Football Stadia Improvement Fund amounting to 70% of the estimated £96,000 cost of re-furbishing the Old Stand and putting crush barriers onto the Covered Terrace. Both structures had been built in the mid-1960s and were showing signs of wear and tear. Without the barriers the terrace's capacity would be reduced to such a level as to bring down the ground's overall capacity to a level that would end in automatic demotion back to the Isthmian League. Work eventually commenced on the refurbishment of the Old Stand and Covered Terrace, completed somewhat later than expected but was finished by December, bringing the capacity back to its former level, the stand formally opened at the end of February 2020.

During the season Hampton lost two of its great servants, Bob Hayes and Alan Duddy. Bob had been Chairman and Patron for nearly 30 years, responsible for dragging Hampton out of the dark days of the early 1990s and into the Isthmian League Premier for the very first time. Alan's history went back even further as a player in the South West Middlesex League days as well as Committee member for many years during the 60s, 70s, 80s and 90s.

National League South: 2019/20 Season

During the summer Chairman Graham Wood handed over the reins to his Vice-Chairman, Jacques le Bars. It had always been intended that when Graham became Chairman two years previously that he would hand over to Jacques (Alan Simpson's God Son) having guided him through the first couple of seasons. Wood was regularly travelling from his home in Sunderland, a 600 mile round trip, which was not sustainable in the long term. However, he became President of the club taking over

Danilo Orsi-Dadomo, Hampton's new goalscoring hero

the mantle of his good friend Alan Simpson. One consequence of this change was that the loss of Wood's financial contribution would have a direct effect on the playing budget for the coming season. Financially the club was sound, but the reality was that without a substantial benefactor or sponsor the club could not commit to the same budget. The Cup run had certainly been beneficial financially, but the club also had to find funds to contribute towards the ground improvements and other off the field costs. Long term financial sustainability was a key objective.

The Beaver's Trust foodbank operation delivers with Trust members Tracey Hathaway and Melissa Gillings

Gary McCann took the news on board and started 'shopping in cheaper markets' bringing in a number of younger, inexperienced players to supplement the team. McCann knew he needed to make wholesale changes but he could now no longer afford the players he had lined up to come in. Only Tyrell Miller Rodney survived from the previous season's squad when Hampton took the long trip to Chelmsford on the opening day of the season. New faces included goalkeeper Laurie Walker on long term loan from MK Dons, Ruaridh Donaldson, a left back who had relocated from Scotland to work in London and previously took the field for Stenhousemuir; Sam Deadfield, a young midfielder who had been captain of Basingstoke Town, Louis Stead, another midfielder from Beaconsfield, Charlie Fox a young central defender just released by QPR; 18 year old Tyrone Lewthwaite, a forward previously with Huddersfield Town; Danilo Orsi-Dadomo, a forward who had played at Hungerford Town; Ed Cook a central defender who had spent some time at Burnley; and Cole Brown and James Ewington, both from Walton Casuals.

Joining them were a few familiar old faces, Dean Inman, Shaun McAuley and Tom Jelley, plus the experienced midfielder Louis Soares just released by Slough Town. Luke Ruddick was retained but was not available for the first game, nor was Shaun McAuley. Ryan Hill could only make the bench. Given so many changes to the squad and budget it was hardly surprising that fans' expectations were more focused on surviving in the league rather than challenging for any honours. With the FA making changes to the structure of non-league, the National League South had only two relegation places, so survival was just a matter of finishing third from bottom.

Chelmsford proved to be the proverbial baptism of fire for the new side. Tom Jelley sliced a clearance into his own goal after just 2 minutes and things went downhill from there. Chelmsford could afford to miss a penalty and still run out 4-1 winners. The first home game was against no less tough opposition, Havant & Waterlooville, who had

Ryan Hill converts his penalty against Hungerford

just been relegated from the Conference National. Gary McCann made a few changes to the side bringing in Brad Pearce and Jude Mason two young defenders on loan from

Sutton Utd. Fans must have been concerned of a repeat of the Chelmsford game when the home side immediately fell behind in the second minute. They fought back to lead 3-1 at half time only to concede three goals in 12 second half minutes to fall short, 3-4. Although Ruddick and McAuley came back into the side from injury results didn't improve until a Sam Deadfield goal earned a 1-0 away win at newly promoted Dorking Wanderers. Nevertheless, it remained a struggle and after 11 games Hampton were rooted to the foot of the table and having to juggle the squad to find a formula that would stem the run of defeats. Then for once the footballing gods smiled on Hampton.

On 1st August Jamal Lowe who had been signed by Portsmouth in October 2016, joined Championship Wigan Athletic for a fee rumoured to be around £3m. Hampton's 15% sell-on clause kicked in. Wigan agreed three staged payments over the next 12 months. The first payment came in in October and it allowed the club to review its player budget and start looking nearer the 'top shelf'.

Hampton's own Flying Scotsman, Ruaridh Donaldson

McCann brought back centre back Charlie Wassmer from Billericay Town initially on loan to provide some 'nous' at the back and he immediately formed a strong paring with Dean Inman. Sam Cox also came back to the club to strengthen the midfield. Right back Matt Young joined from Chelmsford City and midfielder Jake Gray on loan from Woking. Dan Lincoln came in for the error prone Walker between the sticks (Lincoln played cricket for Middlesex during the summer) and much travelled striker Jefferson Louis from Chesham Utd. The defence looked much more solid and there was an upsurge in form with a solid 2-1 F A Cup win at Chesham United. Four league wins out of the next four games eased the Beavers up to 14th and away from immediate relegation danger.

Confidence started to flow back into the side. More new faces came through the Beveree gates, left full back Kyron Farrell, midfielder Wadah Ahmidi and Niko Muir an old Hendon favourite on loan from Hartlepool amongst them. The new attitude showed itself when league leaders Wealdstone came to Beveree and were dispatched 2-0 thanks to goals from Orsi-Dadamo and Jake Gray. It was an amazing turn around but was almost an entirely different team to that which had started the season. The explosion of emotion by the players after the win was not particularly welcomed by the Wealdstone contingent.

On Boxing Day, a 2-1 win was secured at Dulwich Hamlet in front of a 2,089 crowd (Hill and Orsi-Dadomo). During February Hungerford were sent home on the back of a

Niko Muir

7-1 thrashing, followed by a 2-1 win at Dartford. This was followed by a last-minute win at Maidstone United (that man Orsi-Dadomo again netting the winner in the dying seconds). The team was on a roll and by the time New Year came around Hampton were sitting in 9th place and just two points outside the play off places.

Lurking in the background was a menace to health through a virus, initially called Corona but then being known universally as Covid-19. It became apparent that this virus was unknown to science and was proving far more deadly than the 'Flu. The Government were talking of instituting some kind of shutdown affecting Sport/Leisure/Business activities and Schools. No one was quite sure of what was going to happen. As cases rose steeply through late February most sport started to cease on the weekend of 7th/8th March. Going against the trend, the National League instructed its clubs to play on. By March 14th eighth place had been gained, one spot out of the play-offs and just three points behind Dorking Wanderers. Although no one quite knew it at the time, the last league game of the season took place on the 14th March at the Beveree, a draw with Oxford City.

Then, everything stopped. Covid-19 brought an ending not only to football but normal life in general. That last home game against Oxford City was played in an unnatural atmosphere as, virtually, the only football being played in the UK were National League games.

Unlike the previous season there was no romantic FA Cup run but there was a short run in the FA Trophy which saw a 2nd Round trip to NL Premier, Yeovil Town, in January. The Beavers put in a good shift. One down at the break they were still in the tie but conceded a second just after the re-start which all but put the game out of reach. Yeovil showed that a full-time side had too much firepower and won 4-0 in front of a 1,689 crowd in deepest Somerset.

That was it for the 2019/20 season. Stopped in its tracks. What could have ended in another tilt at the play-offs ended not with a shout but with a whimper. Orsi-Dadomo led the way in appearances with 40 (out of a possible 42), followed by Ryan Hill, 39 and Ruaridh Donaldson on 38. Orsi-Dadomo was the main goal threat with 15, surely on course for over 20 in a season, Hill was on 9 when the season was brought to an abrupt end.

The Club was 'mothballed' for the duration – no one knowing how long that would be. The players were put on furlough for the rest of the season and life was locked down.

Months later decisions were made which led to the season being brought to an official close using a 'points per game' system which left the Beavers where they were, 8th, a fraction outside the play-offs. Teams at National League and National North and South lobbied hard to be included as "elite" clubs in line with the Premiership and EFL in order to maintain promotion to the EFL and for promotion and relegation within the National League divisions. There was to be no relegation, however, to Step 3 of the Pyramid as those leagues had been declared null and void.

And so, Wealdstone were declared Champions and promoted. Agreement was reached for play offs to decide the second promotion place – to be played behind closed doors once strict regulations were put in place.

The life of the club did not end entirely for the duration. It was as if the close season had come early. Groundsman, Richard Curtis, continued to work on the pitch. The Club House was decorated internally, as were areas outside. The Foodbank continued to operate with more urgency as the Club, through the Supporters' Trust, became a lifeline to those forced to shield from what appeared to be a deadly virus.

A hiatus ensued, waiting for the news of how life was going to get back to normal. Eventually play offs for the second promotion place were arranged for the end of July – when in normal circumstances the pre-season would be in full swing. Weymouth, who had just been promoted to the Conference South, won through beating Dartford and would take their place in the National League alongside Wealdstone. As regards relegation from the National League only three teams, instead of four, would be relegated (due to the loss of Bury from the English Football League). Ebbsfleet United, AFC Fylde and Chorley were the unlucky teams – Maidenhead escaping the drop in spite of finishing fourth from bottom. Ebbsfleet were to join the South Division which would entail the division running on 21 teams, one short for 2020/21.

Miller-Rodney revives his rivalry with Oldham in the Cup

National League South: 2020/21 Season

Achieving elite status proved to be something of a double-edged sword. The club, and football, entered a strange period of rumour and counter rumour. Decisions made, and then unmade by the governing bodies in reaction to Government announcements that often changed at short notice.

Ryan Hill in action

On the plus side, funding was procured by the National League board from the National Lottery to provide grants to clubs in replacement of lost match day income. Without it very few clubs could afford to even start the season. The first tranche was to replace loss of income up to 31st December. Payments were to be made in relation to a formula worked out by the League in relation to various factors including turnstile income. Needless to say, a number of high rolling clubs were less than satisfied with their allocation as many failed to receive what they thought was adequate compensation. Others were a lot happier and kept quiet.

Elite clubs were allowed to play when the rest of the non-league game was forced to come to a halt as Covid restrictions were imposed during the autumn and winter lockdowns. The downside was that elite clubs were not allowed any spectators whilst Step 3 and below were allowed restricted numbers. Hampton fans got to see a couple of preseason games away from home but otherwise were starved of the opportunity to attend games.

There was an obvious paradox in that clubs with virtually the same support levels at non-league level and very similar ground capacities ended up on either side of an artificial divide, some with fans and some without. Fans from elite clubs were not allowed to attend away matches at non elite clubs (such as the FA Cup and Trophy) - although many did in defiance of the rules. Such was the price of being classified elite. The benefit was that the elite clubs would be able to complete their season, hopefully at some point with fans being readmitted when Covid restrictions were lifted. But just as clubs were allowed to start readmitting fans on a limited basis in the late autumn, the shutters came down again permanently.

Charlie Wassmer

In spite of the ongoing uncertainty Gary McCann was initially able to start building his squad. A bonus was that the majority of the previous season's team was prepared to stay together, a novelty when compared to recent seasons. There was, of course, one or two departures. Leading scorer, Danilo Orsi-Dadomo decided to try his luck with Maidenhead United in the National League, whilst midfielder, Wada Ahmidi, left due to work commitments.

Eventually players were allowed to come together for training with the club carrying out regular temperature checks, and observing social distancing rules, where appropriate. Saturday October 3rd was the date set for a return to competitive football for clubs at Hampton's level, with the F A Cup 2nd Qualifying Round being the first fixture, the competition having already started some weeks before for non-elite teams. Pre-season friendlies could go ahead but, with limited supporters allowed to be present, and preferably no advance advertising of the fixtures.

Hampton carried out changes to the ground, putting in one-way walkways, closing off some of the seating areas (to enable social distancing), installing gangways to enable access to the catering areas and removing all seats and tables from the Clubhouse to make Beveree as Covid secure as possible. The work was carried out by the club's small, but dedicated, band of volunteers.

Alan Julian

A full programme of friendlies was put together by McCann and his management team, though with severe restrictions in place. Any matches played at clubs beneath the National League were allowed limited crowds, however, despite early advice by the government that crowds would also be allowed at National League levels (at a percentage of capacity), this dispensation was then withdrawn in an announcement by Prime Minister, Boris Johnson.

Hampton were then faced with home friendlies against Eastleigh, Sutton United and Woking played behind closed doors. Another serious problem occurred on the eve of the Eastleigh game when Richmond Council advised that the club's safety certificate had been amended and that the attendance level was 'zero'. The only people allowed in the ground apart from the players and management teams were those specifically needed to run the game – initially set at just six persons. It was not until 4pm that afternoon that the club received permission to play matches with a 'temporary' safety certificate issued. The council cited problems associated with Covid (staff working from home) had prevented them in undertaking visits to sporting and other venues and issuing new certificates.

Hampton brought in a number of new players including experienced midfielder Christian Smith from Dulwich Hamlet, left back, Rene Steer from Maidenhead United, and forwards, Nathan Minhas (ex-Bracknell Town) and Danny Bassett from Tooting & Mitcham United. Niko Muir who had joined on loan at the end of the previous season came in on a permanent basis. Also joining was 38 year old goalkeeper, Alan Julian, formerly with Billericay Town (he spent the first few weeks of pre-season known as Triallist 'A', whilst he resolved contractual issues with his former club). Julian lived in the local area and was delighted to have joined his local club, even so late in his career.

The first competitive game of the season was to be the F A Cup 2nd Qualifying Round game at South East Combination, Corinthian, based in North West Kent in front of an all-ticket crowd limited to 300. Corinthian sold tickets within minutes of the draw being made, then on the afternoon of 29th September came a decision by the Football Association that shocked Hampton fans. No supporters from National League clubs would be allowed to attend games – not even at those clubs beneath the NL. The host and visiting clubs were also advised to prevent any Hampton fans from attending. Corinthian were beaten 1-0 in front of a crowd of 221, Ruaridh Donaldson, the scorer. The victory was harder won than it should have been on paper.

Off the field the club also commenced streaming live home games, free of charge and produced an on-line Match Day programme in order to keep connecting with supporters. Season Ticket holders were also offered the chance to request a refund but over 90% decided to allow the club to keep the monies. Given having to go online at such short notice, the club produced remarkably professional coverage and decided unlike most clubs not to charge for the service. An unforeseen benefit of the pandemic was the way that the club upped its efforts in fan engagement not only via match broadcasts but also podcasts and radio coverage keeping the fans updated in what was a bewildering set of circumstances.

Matches continued with full Covid-19 protocols in place, including a penalty shoot-out win over AFC Hornchurch in the 3rd Qualifying Round of the FA Cup, setting up an away draw at fellow South Division, Hemel Hempstead Town. A 1-0 win, with a goal scored by Niko Muir, saw the Beavers through to the 1st Round Proper, for the fourth time– and the second time with McCann in charge. During the Hemel game, what appeared to be a minor collision between Charlie Wassmer and the perimeter wall would see Wassmer out of action until February 6th.

Following the win at Hemel, Ryan Hill, a player who had started to blossom under the guidance of McCann, exercised his option to leave if a higher team came in for him and left to join National League Eastleigh, with the best wishes of everyone at the club. Hill had many admirers for his whole-hearted commitment to the cause. Having started out mainly as a bench-warmer when he joined the club, Hill's obvious ability was not always directed to the right ends. Under Gary McCann he became one of the most exciting players in the division and started to add goals to his game which won him the notice of clubs higher up the Pyramid.

The draw pitted Hampton against Oldham

Gary McCann faces the media

Athletic, now managed by Harry Kewell, a repeat of the tie two years previously - this time, of course, with no supporters allowed into the ground. The game was set for the Sunday 8th, in front of BBC cameras and was shown on BBC iPlayer. As in the previous meeting there was little to separate the two sides, Oldham always just managing to stay ahead. After conceding early, a Sam Deadfield penalty levelled the contest before the Latics took a half time lead. The League 2 team extended their lead soon after half time, but a strike from Deadfield closed the gap. At the end it could be argued that Oldham were hanging on to their lead but in the end won through 3-2. The loss was assuaged by news that the BBC had paid £32,500 to screen the match.

Sam Deadfield concentrates on the penalty for 1-1

The consequence of Wassmer's injury was that the settled back line was disrupted. Dean Inman remained the main pillar of the defence but had to share the pitch with a variety of central defenders; Christian Smith, an oft-injured Luke Ruddick, and Myles Anderson signed on a month-long loan from Weymouth.

Two days later, Hampton returned to league fare with a 1-0 win at table topping Hungerford Town which moved the Beavers up to 11th. The team's form, away from home, improved and wins moved the club up to 4th place. On December 5th supporters were finally allowed into the ground to watch a game – 97 Season Ticket holders were present to watch a 2-0 reverse against St Albans who did the double over Hampton. Following this successful test event, hopes were high for a higher crowd on the next Saturday against Slough Town, however it was not to be. A case of Covid-19 amongst the playing staff led to the postponement of the match and the withdrawal from the FA Trophy as players and management isolated. Then London entered into Tier 3 lockdown on 16th December which meant that, once again, no supporters would be allowed into the ground. A deflating blow for all the work that the club and volunteers had put in.

After the period of self-isolating Hampton bounced back with an impressive win at Dorking Wanderers but then the failings at home re-surfaced with a home loss against Dulwich Hamlet. The Beavers ended 2020 in 5th place in the division, nicely placed in a play-off position.

During this further lockdown McCann continued to bring in players to refresh and improve the squad. Wilson Carvalho, ex-Macclesfield, Ryan Gondoh, from Whyteleafe, David Fisher, AFC Wimbledon and Mauro Vilhete, Wingate & Finchley – players not actively involved in games were more than happy to join a team that was playing and having a measure of success.

The New Year started with a good home performance in a 1-1 draw with Dorking Wanderers before the stop-start effects of the Covid-19 virus kicked in again, this time matches against Slough Town, Concord Rangers and Tonbridge postponed due to outbreaks at those clubs. After a last-minute home win against Ebbsfleet United, the Beavers were then faced with a further delay to the season, related not specifically to Covid-19 but to finance.

Having had a grant from the National Lottery to cover the loss of income for 3 months up to December, it was anticipated that a similar grant would be made for the next period until the end of March. However, the clubs were told by the Government, via the National League board, that there was to be no grant, only loans. The reaction of many clubs, especially in the North and South divisions, was, not surprising, that this was totally unacceptable and if loans had been offered in the first instance very few clubs would have agreed to start the season. Realising that clubs in the two divisions were likely to refuse to play, the National League Board announced a two-week suspension until Friday 5th February, with only the upper division continuing to play on. The National League Board were faced with rebellion and needed time to go back to the Government to try and resolve the situation.

At the beginning of February, the National League issued a number of proposals for the clubs to vote on as to whether or not to keep playing or cancel the season. The clubs were given 28 days to submit their votes. In the meantime, the League indicated that it expected the North and South Division teams to recommence playing on Saturday 6th February. On the day, Hampton travelled to Tonbridge winning 3-0, Wassmer, David Fisher and Donaldson scoring in an impressive performance. On the following Tuesday, 9th, away to Ebbsfleet United in a hastily arranged game, the performance was less impressive, a 2-1 defeat being recorded in what would turn out to be the last game of the season (Fisher scoring again, his third in three games).

Statements from the clubs seemed to be split between bringing the season to an end or carrying on despite the financial implications. It seemed likely that the National League teams would vote to continue whilst the North and South Divisions would vote to null and void the season. On 12th February the Club's Board announced the result of their deliberations and informed supporters that they would, with a heavy heart, vote to null and void the season. Jacques Le Bar, Chairman, gave very clear reasons for the decision…

"Unfortunately, it has become apparent that there will be no positive change in the funding situation and if anything, the landscape has become even more unclear with regards to the proposed loan schemes and their validity within the constitution of the National League itself. After the 3 or 4 years of hard work put in to stabilise the club financially, it would be remiss of us as

custodians to immediately saddle it with a long-term debt commitment, purely to complete a season which in our opinion is now beyond salvation."

Eventually the results of the various votes were declared, the North and South Divisions voting to call time on the season and declare null and void. The National League decided to continue leaving one or two clubs with difficult decisions about whether they could continue or not, seven having voted to stop playing.

Even so, some clubs at North and South level challenged the decision to stop playing and sought to continue via a "mini-league" of those wanting play on in hope of maintaining promotion to the top division. However, their proposal was rejected by the FA Alliance Committee and the Null and Void decision ratified, bringing down the final curtain. At least some degree of certainty was achieved that could allow all clubs to plan properly for a new season, our Centenary Season, to start hopefully the following August.

The stop-start 2020/21 season ended after 21 matches played between October 3rd 2020 and February 9th 2021, possibly the weirdest 129 days in Hampton's history. When the season was suspended Hampton were in 6th position (out of 21 clubs) with 29 points from 17 games and 9 wins, with games in hand over those above them. Only two of those wins came at home with seven away. The lack of supporters at games had clearly had an impact on all levels of football removing the usually assumed home advantage, but it is hard to explain why there should be such a disparity this particular season (although it should be said that the same was an issue in previous seasons with entirely different squads and managers). Having played most of the teams above them and showing excellent form and exuding confidence all around the pitch, there was every expectation of an improvement if the season had gone to its natural end.

Goalkeeper Alan Julian started in every game; Jake Gray appeared in all 21 games (20+1sub). Ruaridh Donaldson, Kyron Farrell, and Niko Muir appeared in 20 games. Muir led the scoring charts with 6, Sam Deadfield, Ryan Gondoh and Donaldson all chipped in with 4.

The 2020/21 season was thought to be done and dusted but early in March there was a surprise in store. The Middlesex FA announced that it had made the draw for the Quarter Finals of the Middlesex Senior Cup. Hampton had been drawn at home to Spelthorne Sports (Combined Counties) and was expected to fulfil the fixture in mid April. The first team players had been put on furlough by the club so the only way to play the fixture was to use the Academy which had just returned to the classroom. The fixture was scheduled for Wednesday April 14th, behind closed doors.

On the player front a number of those who had joined late in the season left the club. Ryan Gondoh (to Wealdstone), Mauro Vilhete (to Dagenham & Redbridge), David Fisher returned to AFC Wimbledon, whilst Wilson Carvalho was on the lookout for full time football. Additionally, Niko Muir went on loan to Woking.

The National League also announced that the North & South Divisions would start their 2021/22 seasons on Saturday August 14th 2021 - all things being equal!

Gary McCann faced a daunting challenge as a manager in three eventful seasons at the Beveree. He showed a determination to carry out his managerial duties despite the pitfalls placed in his way – a lack of players at the beginning of his tenure, budget restraints and a worldwide pandemic. All this and more has tested McCann's ability as a manager to the utmost. Through all this adversity he has built three different teams, created an excellent relationship with his players, shown leadership through crisis and has made it his priority to engage with and communicate with the supporters regardless of any individual result. McCann was never afraid to dodge the questions levied on him in this modern era of Social Media. Some may consider him to be 'old school' in his methods but they have shown that treating everyone as an individual is a benefit to all and will reap benefits on and off the pitch.

With a degree of normality in sight for the forthcoming Centenary season, optimism once again is building for another promotion push with McCann having re-signed the bulk of the previous season's squad, a rare luxury for any non-league manager. A sense of unfinished business is not surprising given the disruption caused by Covid. Promotion to their highest ever level would surely be the icing on the Centenary birthday cake.

Manager's Record

Gary McCann (to date)	P	W	D	L	F	A	Pts	Ave	Win %
Combined	116	50	18	48	156	160			43.1
League	92	36	17	39	124	130	125	1.36	39.1
Cup	24	14	1	9	32	30			58.3

Appendix 1 League Tables

ISTHMIAN LEAGUE PREMIER DIVISION 2002/03

Pos	Team	P	W	D	L	F	A	GD	Pts
1	Aldershot Town	46	33	6	7	81	36	45	105
2	Canvey Island	46	28	8	10	112	56	56	92
3	Hendon	46	22	13	11	70	56	14	79
4	St Albans City	46	23	8	15	73	65	8	77
5	Basingstoke Town	46	23	7	16	80	60	20	76
6	Sutton United	46	22	9	15	77	62	15	75
7	Hayes	46	20	13	13	67	54	13	73
8	Purfleet	46	19	15	12	68	48	20	72
9	Bedford Town	46	21	9	16	66	58	8	72
10	Maidenhead United	46	16	17	13	75	63	12	65
11	Kingstonian	46	16	17	13	71	64	7	65
12	Billericay Town	46	17	11	18	46	44	2	62
13	Bishop's Stortford	46	16	11	19	74	72	2	59
14	HitchinTown	46	15	13	18	69	67	2	58
15	Ford United	46	15	12	19	78	84	-6	57
16	Braintree Town	46	14	12	20	59	71	-12	54
17	Aylesbury United	46	13	15	18	62	75	-13	54
18	Harrow Borough	46	15	9	22	54	75	-21	54
19	Grays Athletic	46	14	11	21	53	59	-6	53
20	Heybridge Swifts	46	13	14	19	52	80	-28	53
21	Chesham United	46	14	10	22	56	81	-25	52
22	Boreham Wood	46	11	15	20	50	58	-8	48
23	Enfield	46	9	11	26	47	101	-54	38
24	HRBFC	46	3	14	29	35	86	-23	23

Aldershot Town promoted to Conference South
Chesham United, Boreham Wood, Enfield & HRBFC relegated

ISTHMIAN LEAGUE DIVISION 1 SOUTH 2003/04

Pos	Team	P	W	D	L	F	A	GD	Pts
1	Lewes	46	29	7	10	113	61	52	94
2	Worthing	46	26	14	6	87	46	41	92
3	Windsor & Eton	46	26	13	7	75	39	36	91
4	Slough Town	46	28	6	12	103	63	40	90
5	HRBFC	46	26	11	9	82	45	37	89
6	Staines Town	46	26	9	11	85	52	33	87
7	Dulwich Hamlet	46	23	15	8	77	57	20	84
8	Bromley	46	22	10	14	80	58	22	76
9	Walton & Hersham	46	20	14	12	76	55	21	74
10	Croydon Athletic	46	20	10	16	70	54	16	70
11	Tooting & Mitcham United	46	20	9	17	82	68	14	69
12	Ashford Town (Middx)	46	18	13	15	69	62	7	67
13	Leatherhead	46	19	9	18	83	88	-5	66
14	Bracknell Town	46	19	6	21	81	87	-6	63
15	Horsham	46	16	11	19	71	69	2	59
16	Marlow	46	16	11	19	50	64	-14	59
17	Whyteleafe	46	17	4	25	66	93	-27	55
18	Banstead Athletic	46	15	8	23	56	73	-17	53
19	Molesey	46	12	6	28	45	84	-39	42
20	Metropolitan Police	46	9	14	23	58	84	-26	41
21	Croydon	46	10	10	26	57	88	-31	40
22	Egham Town	46	8	8	30	55	92	-37	32
23	Corinthian Casuals	46	6	6	34	48	110	-62	24
24	Epsom & Ewell	46	5	8	33	40	117	-77	23

Lewes, Champions, qualified for Play Offs then promoted to Conference South
Worthing, Windsor & Eton, Slough Town, HRBFC and Staines Town promoted to Premier Division
Epsom & Ewell relegated
Ashford Town (Middx), Bracknell Town, Marlow and Egham Town transferred to Southern League

ISTHMIAN LEAGUE PREMIER DIVISION 2004/05

Pos	Team	P	W	D	L	F	A	GD	Pts
1	Yeading	42	25	11	6	74	48	26	86
2	Billericay Town	42	23	11	8	78	40	38	80
3	Eastleigh	42	22	13	7	84	49	35	79
4	Braintree Town	42	19	17	6	67	33	34	74
5	Leyton	42	21	8	13	71	57	14	71
6	HRBFC	42	21	8	13	64	53	11	71
7	Heybridge Swifts	42	18	9	15	76	65	11	63
8	Chelmsford City	42	17	11	14	63	58	5	62
9	Staines Town	42	17	9	16	59	53	6	60
10	Worthing	42	16	11	15	50	45	5	59
11	Hendon	42	17	7	18	48	60	-12	58
12	Salisbury City	42	16	9	17	60	64	-4	57
13	Slough Town	42	15	10	17	61	66	-5	55
14	Folkestone Invicta	42	14	10	18	51	53	-2	52
15	Windsor & Eton	42	12	14	16	48	62	-14	50
16	Harrow Borough	42	13	10	19	41	54	-13	49
17	Northwood	42	14	7	21	49	66	-17	49
18	Wealdstone	42	13	8	21	60	73	-13	47
19	Cheshunt	42	12	11	19	58	71	-13	47
20	Tonbridge Angels	42	11	10	21	47	73	-26	43
21	Dover Athletic	42	10	9	23	50	66	-16	39
22	Kingstonian	42	7	5	30	43	93	-50	26

Yeading promoted as Champions
Eastleigh won Promotion Play-Off Final
Tonbridge Angels, Dover Athletic & Kingstonian relegated
Cheshunt reprieved from relegation (after Hornchurch folded), then transferred to Southern League along with Salisbury City & Northwood

ISTHMIAN LEAGUE PREMIER DIVISION 2005/06

Pos	Team	P	W	D	L	F	A	GD	Pts
1	Braintree Town	42	28	10	4	74	32	42	94
2	Heybridge Swifts	42	28	3	11	70	46	24	87
3	Fisher Athletic	42	26	7	9	84	46	38	85
4	AFC Wimbledon	42	22	11	9	67	36	31	77
5	HRBFC	42	24	3	15	73	54	19	75
6	Staines Town	42	20	10	12	74	56	18	70
7	Billericay Town	42	19	12	11	69	45	24	69
8	Worthing	42	19	10	13	71	60	11	67
9	Walton & Hersham	42	19	7	16	55	50	-5	64
10	Chelmsford City	42	18	10	14	57	62	-5	64
11	Bromley	42	16	14	12	57	49	8	62
12	East Thurrock United	42	18	5	19	60	60	0	59
13	Folkestone Invicta	42	16	10	16	47	51	-4	58
14	Margate	42	11	17	14	49	55	-6	50
15	Leyton	42	13	9	20	58	61	-3	48
16	Harrow Borough	42	13	9	20	56	73	-17	48
17	Slough Town	42	13	8	21	63	75	-12	47
18	Wealdstone	42	13	5	24	68	82	-14	44
19	Hendon	42	9	12	21	44	64	-20	39
20	Maldon Town	42	8	11	23	41	73	-32	35
21	Windsor & Eton	42	8	8	26	37	75	-38	32
22	Redbridge	42	3	5	34	28	97	-69	14

Braintree Town promoted as Champions
Fisher Athletic won Promotion Play-Off Final
Maldon Town, Windsor & Eton and Redbridge relegated
Hendon reprieved from relegation (Canvey Island resigned from Conference)
Wealdstone transferred to Southern League

ISTHMIAN LEAGUE PREMIER DIVISION 2006/07

Pos	Team	P	W	D	L	F	A	GD	Pts	Adj
1	HRBFC	42	24	10	8	77	53	24	82	
2	Bromley	42	23	11	8	83	43	40	80	
3	Chelmsford City	42	23	8	11	96	51	45	77	
4	Billericay Town	42	22	11	9	71	42	29	77	
5	AFC Wimbledon	42	21	15	6	76	37	39	75	-3
6	Margate	42	20	11	11	79	48	31	71	
7	Boreham Wood	42	19	12	11	71	49	22	69	
8	Horsham	42	18	14	10	70	57	13	68	
9	Ramsgate	42	20	5	17	63	63	0	65	
10	Heybridge Swifts	42	17	13	12	57	40	17	64	
11	Tonbridge Angels	42	20	4	18	74	72	2	64	
12	Staines Town	42	15	12	15	64	64	0	57	
13	Carshalton Athletic	42	14	12	16	54	59	-5	54	
14	Hendon	42	16	6	20	53	64	-11	54	
15	Leyton	42	13	10	19	55	77	-22	49	
16	East Thurrock United	42	14	6	22	56	70	-14	48	
17	Ashford Town (Middx)	42	11	13	18	59	71	-12	46	
18	Folkestone Invicta	42	12	10	20	45	66	-21	46	
19	Harrow Borough	42	13	6	23	61	71	-10	45	
20	Worthing	42	8	11	23	57	82	-25	35	
21	Walton & Hersham	42	9	6	27	38	83	-45	33	
22	Slough Town	42	4	6	32	26	123	-97	18	

HRBFC promoted as Champions
Bromley won Promotion Play-Off Final
Worthing, Walton & Hersham and Slough Town relegated
Harrow Borough reprieved from relegation (Hayes & Yeading merged))

FOOTBALL CONFERENCE SOUTH 2007/08

Pos	Team	P	W	D	L	F	A	GD	Pts
1	Lewes	42	27	8	7	81	39	42	89
2	Eastbourne Borough	42	23	11	8	83	38	45	80
3	HRBFC	42	21	14	7	87	49	38	77
4	Fisher Athletic	42	22	5	15	65	61	4	71
5	Braintree Town	42	19	12	11	52	42	10	69
6	Eastleigh	42	19	10	13	76	62	14	67
7	Havant & Waterlooville	42	19	10	13	59	53	6	67
8	Bath City	42	17	15	10	59	36	23	66
9	Newport County	42	18	12	12	64	49	15	66
10	Bishop's Stortford	42	18	10	14	72	60	12	64
11	Bromley	42	19	7	16	77	66	11	64
12	Thurrock	42	18	9	15	63	64	-1	63
13	Hayes & Yeading United	42	14	12	16	67	73	-6	54
14	Cambridge City	42	14	10	18	71	72	-1	52
15	Basingstoke Town	42	12	14	16	54	75	-21	50
16	Welling United	42	13	7	22	41	64	-23	46
17	Maidenhead United	42	11	12	19	56	59	-3	45
18	Bognor Regis Town	42	11	11	20	49	67	-18	44
19	St Albans City	42	10	12	20	43	69	-26	42
20	Weston-super-Mare	42	9	10	23	52	85	-33	37
21	Dorchester Town	42	8	10	24	56	70	-34	34
22	Sutton United	42	5	9	28	32	86	-54	24

Lewes promoted as Champions
Eastbourne Borough won Promotion Play-Off Final
Sutton United relegated
Cambridge City demoted
Dorchester Town reprieved from relegation (Nuneaton Borough, liquidation & Boston United expelled)
Weston-super-Mare reprieved from relegation (Cambridge City, demotion)

FOOTBALL CONFERENCE SOUTH 2008/09

Pos	Team	P	W	D	L	F	A	GD	Pts	Adj
1	AFC Wimbledon	42	26	10	6	86	36	50	88	
2	HRBFC	42	25	10	7	74	37	37	85	
3	Eastleigh	42	25	8	9	69	49	20	83	
4	Hayes & Yeading United	42	24	9	9	74	43	31	81	
5	Chelmsford City	42	23	8	11	72	52	20	77	
6	Maidenhead United	42	21	8	13	57	46	11	71	
7	Welling United	42	19	11	12	61	44	17	68	
8	Bath City	42	20	8	14	56	45	11	68	
9	Bishop's Stortford	42	17	8	17	60	60	0	59	
10	Newport County	42	16	11	15	50	51	-1	59	
11	Team Bath	42	16	7	19	62	64	-2	55	
12	St Albans City	42	14	12	16	56	50	6	54	
13	Bromley	42	15	9	18	60	64	-4	54	
14	Braintree Town	42	14	10	18	57	54	3	52	
15	Havant & Waterlooville	42	11	15	16	59	58	1	48	
16	Worcester City	42	12	11	19	38	53	-15	47	
17	Weston-super-Mare	42	12	11	19	43	68	-25	47	
18	Basingstoke Town	42	10	16	16	36	55	-19	46	
19	Dorchester Town	42	10	12	20	39	61	-22	42	
20	Thurrock	42	9	13	20	54	60	-6	40	
21	Bognor Regis Town	42	7	12	23	33	68	-35	26	-7
22	Fisher Athletic	42	5	3	34	22	100	-78	18	

AFC Wimbledon promoted as Champions
Hayes & Yeading United won Promotion Play-Off Final
Bognor Regis Town relegated
Fisher Athletic folded at the end of the season (as did Team Bath)
Thurrock reprieved from relegation.

FOOTBALL CONFERENCE SOUTH 2009/10

Pos	Team	P	W	D	L	F	A	GD	Pts
1	Newport County	42	32	7	3	93	26	67	103
2	Dover Athletic	42	22	9	11	66	47	19	75
3	Chelmsford City	42	22	9	11	62	48	14	75
4	Bath City	42	20	12	10	66	46	20	72
5	Woking	42	21	9	12	57	44	13	72
6	Havant & Waterlooville	42	19	14	9	65	44	21	71
7	Braintree Town	42	18	17	7	56	41	15	71
8	Staines Town	42	18	13	11	59	40	19	67
9	Welling United	42	18	9	15	66	51	15	63
10	Thurrock	42	16	13	13	66	60	6	61
11	Eastleigh	42	17	9	16	71	66	5	60
12	Bromley	42	15	10	17	68	64	4	55
13	St Albans City	42	15	10	17	45	55	-10	55
14	HRBFC	42	14	9	19	56	66	-10	51
15	Basingstoke Town	42	13	10	19	49	68	-19	49
16	Maidenhead United	42	12	12	18	52	59	-7	48
17	Dorchester Town	42	13	9	20	56	74	-18	48
18	Bishop's Stortford	42	12	11	19	48	59	-11	47
19	Lewes	42	9	15	18	49	63	-14	42
20	Worcester City	42	10	10	22	48	60	-12	40
21	Weston-super-Mare	42	5	8	29	48	93	-45	23
22	Weymouth	42	5	7	30	31	103	-72	22

Newport County promoted as Champions
Bath City won Promotion Play-Off Final
Weymouth relegated
Worcester City & West-super-Mare reprieved from relegation (National League Salisbury City demoted two levels)
Worcester City subsequently transferred to Conference North

FOOTBALL CONFERENCE SOUTH 2010/11

Pos	Team	P	W	D	L	F	A	GD	Pts
1	Braintree Town	42	27	8	7	78	33	45	89
2	Farnborough	42	25	7	10	83	47	36	82
3	Ebbsfleet United	42	22	12	8	75	51	24	78
4	Chelmsford City	42	23	8	11	82	50	32	77
5	Woking	42	22	10	10	62	42	20	76
6	Welling United	42	24	8	10	81	47	34	75
7	Dover Athletic	42	22	8	12	80	51	29	74
8	Eastleigh	42	22	6	14	74	53	21	72
9	Havant & Waterlooville	42	16	10	16	56	51	5	58
10	Dartford	42	15	12	15	60	59	1	57
11	Bromley	42	15	12	15	49	61	-12	57
12	Weston-super-Mare	42	15	8	19	56	67	-11	53
13	Basingstoke Town	42	13	10	19	50	63	-13	49
14	Boreham Wood	42	12	11	19	56	67	-11	47
15	Staines Town	42	11	14	17	48	63	-15	47
16	Bishop's Stortford	42	13	6	23	48	79	-31	45
17	Dorchester Town	42	10	14	18	49	59	-10	44
18	HRBFC	42	9	15	18	43	61	-18	42
19	Maidenhead United	42	10	10	22	43	70	-27	40
20	Thurrock	42	8	13	21	50	77	-27	37
21	Lewes	42	9	9	24	34	70	-36	36
22	St Albans City	42	7	13	22	39	75	-36	24

Braintree Town promoted as Champions
Ebbsfleet United won Promotion Play-Off Final
Lewes & St Albans City relegated
Thurrock reprieved from relegation after Rushden & Diamonds expelled from Conference
Bishop's Stortford transferred to Conference North

FOOTBALL CONFERENCE SOUTH 2011/12

Pos	Team	P	W	D	L	F	A	GD	Pts
1	Woking	42	30	7	5	92	41	51	97
2	Dartford	42	26	10	6	89	39	50	88
3	Welling United	42	24	9	9	79	47	32	81
4	Sutton United	42	20	14	8	68	53	15	74
5	Basingstoke Town	42	20	11	11	65	50	15	71
6	Chelmsford City	42	18	15	11	66	45	21	69
7	Dover Athletic	42	17	15	10	62	48	14	66
8	Boreham Wood	42	17	10	15	66	58	8	61
9	Tonbridge Angels	42	15	12	15	70	67	3	57
10	Salisbury City	42	15	12	15	55	54	1	57
11	Dorchester Town	42	16	9	18	58	65	-7	57
12	Eastleigh	42	15	9	18	57	63	-6	54
13	Weston-super-Mare	42	14	9	19	58	71	-13	51
14	Farnborough	42	15	6	21	52	79	-27	51
15	Staines Town	42	12	12	19	54	63	-9	48
16	Truro City	42	13	9	20	65	80	-15	48
17	Bromley	42	10	15	17	52	66	-14	45
18	Eastbourne Borough	42	12	9	21	54	69	-15	45
19	Maidenhead United	42	11	10	21	49	74	-25	43
20	Havant & Waterlooville	42	10	12	20	62	75	-13	42
21	HRBFC	42	10	12	20	53	68	-15	42
22	Thurrock	42	5	11	26	33	84	-51	26

Woking promoted as Champions
Dartford won Promotion Play-Off Final
HRBFC & Thurrock relegated

ISTHMIAN LEAGUE PREMIER DIVISION 2012/13

Pos	Team	P	W	D	L	F	A	GD	Pts
1	Whitehawk	42	25	13	4	88	42	46	88
2	Lowestoft Town	42	23	11	8	71	38	33	80
3	Wealdstone	42	22	13	7	70	38	32	79
4	Concord Rangers	42	22	10	10	80	54	26	76
5	East Thurrock United	42	18	16	8	65	45	20	70
6	Metropolitan Police	42	20	10	12	65	56	9	70
7	Bury Town	42	19	9	14	66	64	2	66
8	Canvey Island	42	18	10	14	60	55	5	64
9	Margate	42	17	11	14	61	49	12	62
10	Hendon	42	16	12	14	48	50	-2	60
11	Kingstonian	42	18	5	19	63	62	1	59
12	Leiston	42	13	17	12	55	57	-2	56
13	HRBFC	42	13	14	15	58	56	2	53
14	Bognor Regis Town	42	15	8	19	48	58	-10	53
15	Harrow Borough	42	12	9	21	53	71	-18	45
16	Enfield Town	42	13	5	24	60	83	-23	44
17	Cray Wanderers	42	10	13	19	60	85	-25	43
18	Wingate & Finchley	42	12	6	24	56	82	-26	42
19	Lewes	42	9	13	20	59	75	-16	40
20	Carshalton Athletic	42	12	4	26	55	76	-21	40
21	Hastings United	42	8	15	19	39	62	-23	39
22	Thurrock	42	11	8	23	40	62	-22	38

Whitehawk promoted as Champions
Concord Rangers won Promotion Play-Off Final
Hastings United & Thurrock relegated

ISTHMIAN LEAGUE PREMIER DIVISION 2013/14

Pos	Team	P	W	D	L	F	A	GD	Pts
1	Wealdstone	46	28	12	6	99	43	56	96
2	Kingstonian	46	25	10	11	80	44	36	85
3	Bognor Regis Town	46	26	7	13	95	65	30	85
4	Lowestoft Town	46	24	12	10	76	40	36	84
5	AFC Hornchurch	46	24	11	11	83	53	30	83
6	Dulwich Hamlet	46	25	7	14	96	65	31	82
7	Maidstone United	46	23	12	11	92	57	35	81
8	Hendon	46	21	7	18	84	69	15	70
9	Leiston	46	19	10	17	73	71	2	67
10	Billericay Town	46	19	9	18	66	64	2	66
11	Margate	46	18	10	18	70	67	3	64
12	HRBFC	46	18	10	18	72	70	2	64
13	Canvey Island	46	17	11	18	65	65	0	62
14	Grays Athletic	46	17	10	19	74	82	-8	61
15	Bury Town	46	17	9	20	60	65	-5	60
16	Lewes	46	14	17	15	67	67	0	59
17	Metropolitan Police	46	15	13	18	58	59	-1	58
18	Harrow Borough	46	15	13	18	66	72	-6	58
19	Enfield Town	46	13	12	21	64	90	-26	51
20	East Thurrock United	46	13	10	23	66	84	-18	49
21	Wingate & Finchley	46	14	7	25	57	84	-27	49
22	Thamesmead Town	46	12	10	24	61	90	-29	46
23	Carshalton Athletic	46	8	6	32	40	101	-61	30
24	Cray Wanderers	46	7	3	34	40	137	-97	26

Wealdstone promoted as Champions
Lowestoft Town won Promotion Play-Off Final
Thamesmead Town, Carshalton Athletic & Cray Wanderers relegated
Wingate & Finchley reprieved (due to Worksop Town resigning from the Northern Premier League)

ISTHMIAN LEAGUE PREMIER DIVISION 2014/15

Pos	Team	P	W	D	L	F	A	GD	Pts	Adj
1	Maidstone United	46	29	11	6	85	41	44	98	
2	Hendon	46	27	14	5	82	55	27	95	
3	Margate	46	25	10	11	94	58	36	85	
4	Dulwich Hamlet	46	21	13	12	66	51	15	76	
5	Metropolitan Police	46	21	12	13	72	51	21	75	
6	Grays Athletic	46	22	8	16	70	57	13	74	
7	Enfield Town	46	24	4	18	70	56	14	73	-3
8	Billericay Town	46	20	8	18	73	65	8	68	
9	Leiston	46	18	13	15	73	58	15	67	
10	Leatherhead	46	19	10	17	72	62	10	67	
11	Kingstonian	46	18	13	15	63	56	7	67	
12	Wingate & Finchley	46	20	7	19	72	70	2	67	
13	East Thurrock United	46	17	15	14	66	71	-5	66	
14	Bognor Regis Town	46	17	12	17	71	64	7	63	
15	HRBFC	46	16	9	21	62	79	-17	57	
16	Harrow Borough	46	15	8	23	64	77	-13	53	
17	Canvey Island	46	14	11	21	61	77	-16	53	
18	VCD Athletic	46	14	11	21	53	70	-17	53	
19	Lewes	46	14	11	21	45	67	-22	53	
20	Tonbridge Angels	46	13	13	20	63	67	-4	52	
21	Peacehaven & Telscombe	46	13	9	24	58	85	-27	48	
22	Witahm Town	46	9	15	22	61	84	-23	42	
23	AFC Hornchurch	46	10	10	26	46	70	-24	40	
24	Bury Town	46	7	11	28	35	86	-51	32	

Maidstone United promoted as Champions
Margate won Promotion Play-Off Final
Peacehaven & Telscombe, Witham Town, AFC Hornchurch & Bury Town relegated

ISTHMIAN LEAGUE PREMIER DIVISION 2015/16

Pos	Team	P	W	D	L	F	A	GD	Pts
1	HRBFC	46	28	11	7	105	52	53	95
2	Bognor Regis Town	46	29	7	10	95	42	53	94
3	East Thurrock United	46	26	13	7	107	53	54	91
4	Tonbridge Angels	46	24	13	9	90	49	41	85
5	Dulwich Hamlet	46	23	12	11	93	58	35	81
6	Enfield Town	46	24	8	14	74	47	27	80
7	Kingstonian	46	21	10	15	78	64	14	73
8	Leiston	46	20	12	14	72	57	15	72
9	Billericay Town	46	18	17	11	76	53	23	71
10	Merstham	46	18	8	20	74	80	-6	62
11	Leatherhead	46	18	8	20	67	81	-14	62
12	Metropolitan Police	46	17	10	19	60	79	-19	61
13	Wingate & Finchley	46	17	9	20	66	70	-4	60
14	Canvey Island	46	17	9	20	69	89	-20	60
15	Grays Athletic	46	15	12	19	63	74	-11	57
16	Staines Town	46	15	10	21	53	74	-21	55
17	Harrow Borough	46	15	9	22	66	80	-14	54
18	Farnborough	46	16	5	25	65	88	-23	53
19	Hendon	46	13	13	20	68	85	-17	52
20	Needham Market	46	13	12	21	51	76	-25	51
21	Burgess Hill Town	46	12	14	20	57	73	-16	50
22	Brentwood Town	46	10	10	26	51	80	-29	40
23	Lewes	46	6	16	24	48	87	-39	34
24	VCD Athletic	46	8	10	28	46	103	-57	31

Hampton & Richmond Borough promoted as Champions
East Thurrock United won Promotion Play-Off Final
Brentwood Town, Lewes & VCD Athletic relegated
Farnborough demoted

NATIONAL LEAGUE SOUTH 2016/17

Pos	Team	P	W	D	L	F	A	GD	Pts
1	Maidenhead United	42	30	8	4	93	29	64	98
2	Ebbsfleet United	42	29	9	4	96	30	66	96
3	Dartford	42	25	9	8	83	45	38	84
4	Chelmsford City	42	23	13	6	89	47	42	82
5	Poole Town	42	20	11	11	63	49	14	71
6	Hungerford Town	42	19	10	10	67	49	18	70
7	HRBFC	42	19	11	11	81	56	25	69
8	Wealdstone	42	18	12	12	62	58	4	66
9	Bath City	42	18	16	16	71	52	19	62
10	St Albans City	42	16	15	15	72	66	6	59
11	Eastbourne Borough	42	16	16	16	82	70	12	58
12	Hemel Hempstead Town	42	15	15	15	74	83	-9	57
13	East Thurrock United	42	14	14	14	73	65	8	56
14	Oxford City	42	15	7	20	48	73	-25	52
15	Weston-super-Mare	42	14	6	22	63	69	-6	48
16	Welling United	42	12	7	23	64	69	-5	43
17	Whitehawk	42	12	7	23	51	72	-21	43
18	Concord Rangers	42	10	12	20	57	75	-18	42
19	Truro City	42	11	7	24	53	99	-46	40
20	Gosport Borough	42	9	9	24	45	101	-56	36
21	Bishop's Stortford	42	8	3	31	29	104	-75	27
22	Margate	42	7	4	31	26	81	-55	25

Maidenhead United promoted as Champions
Ebbsfleet United won Promotion Play-Off Final
Poole Town, Hungerford Town & Wealdstone excluded from Play Offs due to ground grading issues. HRBFC took part in play-offs.
Gosport Borough, Bishop's Stortford & Margate relegated

NATIONAL LEAGUE SOUTH 2017/18

Pos	Team	P	W	D	L	F	A	GD	Pts	Adj
1	Havant & Waterlooville	42	25	11	6	70	30	40	86	
2	Dartford	42	26	8	8	81	44	37	86	
3	Chelmsford City	42	21	11	10	68	45	23	74	
4	HRBFC	42	18	18	6	58	37	21	72	
5	Hemel Hempstead Town	42	19	13	10	71	51	20	70	
6	Braintree Town	42	19	13	10	73	55	18	69	-1
7	Truro City	42	20	9	13	71	55	16	69	
8	St Albans City	42	19	8	15	71	58	13	65	
9	Bath City	42	17	12	13	64	48	16	63	
10	Welling United	42	17	10	15	68	59	9	61	
11	Wealdstone	42	16	11	15	64	62	2	59	
12	Weston-super-Mare	42	16	7	19	66	73	-7	55	
13	Chippenham Town	42	15	9	18	64	70	-6	54	
14	Gloucester City	42	15	8	19	56	70	-14	53	
15	East Thurrock United	42	13	11	18	68	84	-16	50	
16	Oxford City	42	13	10	19	60	69	-9	49	
17	Concord Rangers	42	12	10	20	46	62	-16	46	
18	Eastbourne Borough	42	13	7	22	57	80	-23	46	
19	Hungerford Town	42	12	7	23	45	68	-23	43	
20	Poole Town	42	11	9	22	47	73	-26	42	
21	Whitehawk	42	8	10	24	51	89	-38	34	
22	Bognor Regis Town	42	5	12	25	41	78	-37	27	

Havant & Waterlooville promoted as Champions
Braintree Town won Promotion Play-Off Final
Poole Town, Whitehawk & Bognor Regis Town relegated

NATIONAL LEAGUE SOUTH 2018/19

Pos	Team	P	W	D	L	F	A	GD	Pts	Adj
1	Torquay United	42	27	7	8	93	41	52	88	
2	Woking	42	23	9	10	76	49	27	78	
3	Welling United	42	23	7	12	70	47	23	76	
4	Chelmsford City	42	21	9	12	68	50	18	72	
5	Bath City	42	20	11	11	58	36	22	71	
6	Concord Rangers	42	20	13	9	69	48	21	70	-3
7	Wealdstone	42	18	12	12	62	50	12	66	
8	Billericay Town	42	19	8	15	72	65	7	65	
9	St Albans City	42	18	10	14	67	64	3	64	
10	Dartford	42	18	10	14	52	58	-6	64	
11	Slough Town	42	17	12	13	56	50	6	63	
12	Oxford City	42	17	5	20	64	63	1	56	
13	Chippenham Town	42	16	7	19	57	64	-7	55	
14	Dulwich Hamlet	42	13	10	19	52	65	-13	49	
15	HRBFC	42	13	10	19	49	66	-17	49	
16	Hemel Hempstead Town	42	12	12	18	52	67	-15	48	
17	Gloucester City	42	12	11	19	35	54	-19	47	
18	Eastbourne Borough	42	10	12	20	32	65	-13	42	
19	Hungerford Town	42	11	9	22	45	72	-27	42	
20	Truro City	42	9	12	21	63	87	-24	39	
21	East Thurrock United	42	10	7	25	42	63	-21	37	
22	Weston-super-Mare	42	8	11	23	50	80	-30	35	

Torquay United promoted as Champions
Woking won Promotion Play-Off Final
Truro City, East Thurrock United & Weston-super-Mare relegated

NATIONAL LEAGUE SOUTH 2019/20

Pos	Team	P	W	D	L	F	A	GD	Pts	PPG
1	Wealdstone	33	22	4	7	69	35	34	70	89.09
2	Havant & Waterlooville	34	19	10	5	64	37	27	67	82.77
3	Weymouth	35	17	12	6	60	35	25	63	75.6
4	Bath City	35	18	9	8	50	37	13	63	75.6
5	Slough Town	35	17	9	9	51	38	13	60	72
6	Dartford	34	16	8	10	60	46	14	56	69.18
7	Dorking Wanderers	35	14	8	13	58	56	2	50	60
8	HRBFC	33	14	5	14	51	50	1	47	59.82
9	Maidstone United	33	12	9	12	48	44	4	45	57.27
10	Chelmsford City	34	11	11	12	55	56	-1	44	54.4
11	Hemel Hempstead Town	34	12	8	14	36	43	-7	44	54.4
12	Welling United	34	12	6	16	38	46	-8	42	51.9
13	Oxford City	34	11	9	14	47	60	-13	42	51.9
14	Chippenham Town	35	10	12	13	39	45	-6	42	50.4
15	Tonbridge Angels	31	9	9	13	46	54	-8	36	48,78
16	Concord Rangers	32	10	7	15	44	48	-4	37	48.56
17	Billericay Town	32	8	13	11	46	55	-9	37	48.56
18	Eastbourne Borough	33	8	14	11	38	54	-16	38	48.36
19	Dulwich Hamlet	35	9	10	16	51	50	1	37	44.4
20	St Albans City	35	9	10	16	41	54	-13	37	44.4
21	Braintree Town	35	10	5	20	44	67	-23	35	42
22	Hungerford Town	33	8	4	21	38	64	-26	28	35.64

Season declared null & void.
Wealdstone declared Champions and promoted to National League
League places decided by Points per Game calculation.
Weymouth promoted after winning Play-Off Final.
No relegation.

NATIONAL LEAGUE SOUTH 2020/21

Pos	Team	P	W	D	L	F	A	GD	Pts
1	Dorking Wanderers	18	12	3	3	40	17	23	39
2	Dartford	19	10	4	5	26	17	9	34
3	Eastbourne Borough	19	9	6	4	36	26	10	33
4	Oxford City	17	9	5	3	35	17	18	32
5	St Albans City	15	9	5	1	22	10	12	32
6	HRBFC	17	9	2	6	24	16	8	29
7	Hungerford Town	19	9	2	8	27	28	-1	29
8	Ebbsfleet United	18	8	4	6	26	24	2	28
9	Havant & Waterlooville	14	6	2	6	25	21	4	20
10	Hemel Hempstead Town	18	6	2	10	28	38	-10	20
11	Maidstone United	13	5	4	4	24	18	6	19
12	Dulwich Hamlet	13	4	4	5	15	17	-2	16
13	Chelmsford City	16	4	4	8	21	25	-4	16
14	Tonbridge Angels	14	5	1	8	16	23	-7	16
15	Billericay Town	17	4	4	9	26	35	-9	16
16	Chippenham Town	14	4	4	6	13	22	-9	16
17	Concord Rangers	14	3	5	6	16	24	-8	14
18	Bath City	13	4	1	8	16	23	-7	13
19	Braintree Town	16	4	1	11	19	34	-15	13
20	Slough Town	12	3	3	6	16	24	-8	12
21	Welling United	14	2	6	6	18	30	-12	12

National League (North & South) season declared null and void after vote by National League Clubs
No promotion or relegation

Appendix 2   Club Honours 1959 to date (as a Senior Club)

SURREY SENIOR LEAGUE
Champions; 1963/64
League Cup Finalists; 1960/61

SPARTAN LEAGUE
Champions; 1964/65, 1965/66, 1966/67, 1969/70
League Cup Winners; 1964/65, 1965/66, 1966/67, 1967/68
League Cup Finalists; 1968/69, 1969/70

ISTHMIAN LEAGUE
Champions; 2006/07, 2015/16
League Cup Finalists; 2001/02, 2004/05
Play Off Finalists; 2005/06
Charity Shield Winners; 2016/17

FOOTBALL CONFERENCE/NATIONAL LEAGUE
South Division
Play Off Finalists; 2007/08, 2008/09, 2017/18

MIDDLESEX SENIOR CUP
Winners; 2005/06, 2007/08, 2011/12, 2013/14, 2016/17
Finalists; 1971/72, 1976/77, 1995/96, 2004/05

LONDON SENIOR CUP
Finalists; 1986/87, 1987/88

MIDDLESEX SENIOR CHARITY CUP
Winners; 1969/70, 1995/96, 1997/98, 1998/99
Finalists; 1968/69, 1971/72, 1972/73, 1989/90, 1994/95

MIDDLESEX SUPER CUP (George Ruffell Trophy)
Winners; 199/2000, 2006/07

SOUTHERN COMBINATION CUP
Winners; 1968/69, 1971/72, 1976/77, 1981/82, 1983/84, 1996/97
Finalists; 1972/73, 1977/78, 1979/80, 1997/98

1921 to 1959 (as a Junior Club)
Not a complete record

KINGSTON & DISTRICT LEAGUE
Champions; 1929/30, 1930/31, 1931/32, 1932/33

KINGSTON SENIOR LEAGUE CUP
Winners; 1928/29 (Shared Trophy), 1929/30 (Shared Trophy), 1930/31, 1931/32, 1932/33
Finalists;

MIDDLESEX JUNIOR CUP
Winners; 1931/32
Finalists;

MIDDLESEX JUNIOR CHARITY CUP
Winners; 1931/32
Finalists; 1928/29

BLAIR SENIOR CHARITY CUP
Winners; 1928/29, 1930/31, 1931/32, 1932/33, 1938/39
Finalists; 1927/28,

HAMPTON HOSPITAL CUP
Winners; 1932/33
Finalists;

RICHMOND CHALLENGE CUP
Winners; 1958/59
Finalists;

RIDGE CUP
Winners; 1930/31, 1932/33
Finalists; 1931/32

SOUTH WEST MIDDLESEX VICTORY CUP
Winners; 1947/48, 1953/54
Finalists; 1923/24, 1935/36, 1950/51, 1956/57

TECK SENIOR CUP
Winners; 1925/26, 1930/31, 1931/32, 1936/37
Finalists; 1929/30

TWICKENHAM CHARITY CUP
Winners; 1937/38
Finalists;

Appendix 3

100 Club: players making 100 or more appearances 2002-21

	Started	Sub	Total	Era	All Time Ranking
Dean WELLS	332	5	337	2004 - 2011	8
Matt LOVETT	295	0	295	2005 - 2012	12
Lawrence YAKU	205	71	276	2005 - 2011	15
Orlando JEFFREY	263	9	272	2003 - 2011	17
Alan INNS	245	22	267	2002 - 2008	19=
Charlie MOONE	202	55	257	2010 - 2016	23
Barrie MATTHEWS	201	52	253	2005 - 2011	24=
Marcello FERNANDES	197	55	252	2003 - 2010	26
Graham HARPER	236	13	249	2004 - 2011	27
Dudley GARDNER	168	74	242	1998 - 2008	29
Ian HODGES	158	33	191	2006 - 2011	36
Nathan COLLIER	173	14	187	2009 - 2017	37=
Stuart LAKE	152	29	181	2006 - 2014	43
James SIMMONDS	150	28	178	2009 - 2015	44
Elliott GODFREY	148	28	176	2004 - 2008	45
Dean INMAN	156	10	166	2008 - to date	50
Shaun McAULEY	99	61	160	2007 - 2020	57
Josh CASEY	150	6	156	2015 - 2018	58
Rob PARIS	144	10	154	2003 - 2008	60
Francis QUARM	136	11	147	2005 - 2011	65=
Dave TARPEY	108	39	147	2009 - 2014	66
Darren POWELL	133	13	146	1996 - 2014	68
Andy MORLEY	125	10	135	2003 - 2006	80
Brendan KIERNAN	120	14	134	2015 - 2018	83
Ryan LAKE	99	25	124	2005 - 2009	88
Joe TURNER	103	20	123	2011 - 2014	89
Rodney CHIWESHE	121	0	121	2011 - 2014	91
Tom JELLEY	110	10	120	2015 - 2019	94
Richard O'CONNOR	90	28	118	2001 - 2005	96
Matt ELVERSON	100	11	111	2004 - 2007	98
George WELLS	96	11	107	2012 - 2015	101
Kieran MURPHY	102	3	105	2014 - 2017	104
Gary HOLLOWAY	100	4	104	2000 - 2013	105
Michael KAMARA	83	18	101	2015 - 2018	110

Printed in Great Britain
by Amazon